# The Lilies and the T̲h̲i̲s̲t̲l̲e̲

## French Troops in the Jacobite '45

Andrew Bamford

Helion & Company

Helion & Company Limited
Unit 8 Amherst Business Centre
Budbrooke Road
Warwick
CV34 5WE
England
Tel. 0121 705 3393
Fax 0121 711 4075
Email: info@helion.co.uk
Website: www.helion.co.uk
Twitter: @helionbooks
Visit our blog at http://blog.helion.co.uk/

Published by Helion & Company 2018
Designed and typeset by Mach 3 Solutions Ltd (www.mach3solutions.co.uk)
Cover designed by Paul Hewitt, Battlefield Design (www.battlefield-design.co.uk)
Printed by Henry Ling Limited, Dorchester

Text © Andrew Bamford 2018
Cover: 'Advance of the composite French battalion at Falkirk, 17 January 1746', original artwork by
Steve Noon, © Helion & Company 2018
Uniform plates by Mark Allen, © Helion & Company 2018; other images as credited

Every reasonable effort has been made to trace copyright holders and to obtain their permission
for the use of copyright material. The author and publisher apologise for any errors or omissions in
this work, and would be grateful if notified of any corrections that should be incorporated in future
reprints or editions of this book.

ISBN 978-1-911628-17-0

British Library Cataloguing-in-Publication Data.
A catalogue record for this book is available from the British Library.

For details of other military history titles published by Helion & Company Limited, contact the
above address, or visit our website: http://www.helion.co.uk

We always welcome receiving book proposals from prospective authors.

To the soldiers of the Régiment de Dillon – past and present

# Contents

Introduction                                        vii

1   Backing the Rising                               11
2   Regiments and Soldiers                           30
3   Uniforms and Equipment                           56
4   French Troops in Scotland                        70
5   After the Rising                                103

Notes on the Plates                                113
Bibliography                                       117

# Introduction

One of the best things to have come out of the last couple of decades of scholarship on the Jacobite rising of 1745 is the recognition that these events were not part of a British civil war, nor even, as older accounts and nationalist zealots would have it, a conflict between England and Scotland, but a small part in a series of interlinked global conflicts that stretched out over much of the globe. In this light, Christopher Duffy is in particular to be praised for drawing attention to the role of Hessian forces in the suppression of the Rising and, of course, the British Government also made use of Dutch auxiliaries to supplement its forces which is a topic that still merits a detailed study. That said, however, there has been little attention during this time to the role of French military and naval forces during the campaign. The French political involvement and the place of the '45 in French grand strategy are, it is true, covered in exhaustive detail in McLynn's 1981 *France and the Jacobite Rising of 1745*, but the scope and focus of McLynn's book prevent him going into detail on organisational, operational, and tactical matters. More recent studies of the armies and battles of the '45 have brought out the roles of French forces at Inverurie, Falkirk, and Culloden with varying degrees of detail and accuracy but there has until now been no single work focused upon the French contribution.

The attention of this work, therefore, is several-fold. Firstly, to place the events of 1745 and 1746 into the context of French grand strategy or in order to bring out how and why France became as heavily involved in the Rising as she did (and, also, why this involvement did not develop even further in the way that many Jacobites hoped it would). Necessarily, much of this narrative will draw on McLynn's existing work, but it forms an essential context for what follows.

Secondly, to look at the role of French naval forces in events, from the initial expedition that landed Prince Charles Edward Stuart and his companions at Moidart, through the attempts to supply manpower and material to the burgeoning rising, to the eventual rescue of the Prince and those of his followers who were able to make their escape. It would be fair to say that without this maritime lifeline, risky though it was, the Rising would likely never have taken place and certainly could not have progressed in the way that it did.

Thirdly, to address the role of French support of the Jacobite army in the broadest sense, both logistically and in terms of the support offered by specialist officers both at an army and a unit level.

Fourthly, to explore the nature and origins of the French forces deployed to Scotland, the bulk of whom, of course, were members of the French army's famed Irish Brigade and the associated Régiment Royal Ecossois. In the aftermath of the rising, the British authorities were very keen to uncover the origins of the men in the ranks of these units, and their investigations into the prisoners who fell into their hands offer new insights into the nationalities and origins of these men and the circumstances of their enlistment and service.

Fifthly, since the dress and appearance of the French troops involved in the campaign has become confused and romanticised over the years, to detail the uniforms and equipment of the troops deployed to Scotland and address a number of misconceptions and exaggerations which have made their way into print on this topic.

Sixthly, to provide an overview of the role of French units in the campaign and an assessment of their contribution to the Jacobite military effort, and, lastly, to consider the post-1746 role of the French army as a home for those forced to flee into exile as a result of the Jacobite failure.

It is hoped that all the terminology employed in this work is clear enough to be readily understood, but where there is any doubt then a potentially-confusing term has been explained when first encountered. One point that is worth addressing now, though, is the question of dates. France at this time employed the modern Gregorian Calendar whereas Britain had thus far refused to have any truck with such popish meddling and stuck to the older Julian Calendar which was 11 days adrift by the mid-18th century. Since the bulk of the narrative element of this book takes place in the British Isles, the older form of dating has been employed; when the French dating has been used, as for example in the account of naval operations and events on the Continent, this has been indicated by the addition of (NS), for new style, after the date. The British convention of starting the New Year on Lady Day (25 March) has, however, been ignored. Additionally, as befitting the French ambivalence on the matter of who was the lawful monarch of Great Britain, it should be noted that I have accorded royal titles to the members of both the House of Hanover and the House of Stuart.

As ever, although the book has my name on the front cover its contents owe a great deal to those who have helped me along the way. Uniform historian David Wilson was of great assistance in sharing with me his drafts for what he plans to be the definitive account of the uniforms of the French army in the 1740s, and was of particular help when it came to the details of the Régiment Royal Ecossois of which he has made a particular study. Similarly, Pierre-Louis Coudray was kind enough to take some time to share his research into the social history of the Irish Brigade and its historical reputation, following a fascinating paper on that topic at the 2017 New Research Conference hosted by the British Commission for Military History. Laura Short very kindly shared with me archival transcriptions collected as part of a dissertation on this topic, many of which were translated into

English by her mother-in-law which saved me a substantial amount of work. Jonathan Oates also shared his research into the role of the French contingent at Falkirk, gathered as part of his research for a new history of that battle, and Albert Parker was of great assistance in reconciling conflicting details with respect to the naval elements of the campaign.

Much of the archival work that underpins Chapter 2 was undertaken at The National Archives in Kew, and the staff there were their usual helpful selves. In terms of archival support, I must also thank the staff of the Picture Library, National Museums Scotland, for their help in providing an image of the beautiful – if controversial – Royal Ecossois grenadier cap in their collection.

For anyone who might assume that as commissioning editor for Helion with responsibility for the 'From Reason to Revolution' series I can circumvent the usual processes and publish such of my own writing as I see fit, I must, alas, disabuse them of this belief. I must therefore thank Helion director Duncan Rogers for approving the project, for allowing me the time and flexibility to complete this work alongside my regular job, and for assisting in locating rare sources. Being naturally unable to copy-edit my own work, I must thank Serena Jones for taking on that role, and Kim McSweeney for creating the finished book. Nor would the work be anything like as impressive were it not for the beautiful artwork that was done to accompany it, and I must therefore also express my appreciation to Steve Noon for the magnificent centrepiece painting which also graces the cover, and Mark Allen for the uniform plates which form the backbone of the colour section.

Lastly, I should thank the many and varied members of the mildly eccentric and decidedly international community who devote their spare time to re-enacting the armies of 1745 at sites throughout the British Isles and who I am proud to count amongst my friends. My initial interest in the French role in the events of 1745 came through my involvement in this community, leading to the decision with a group of like-minded fellows to begin our own recreation of some of these troops. That decision was made over a decade ago now – in a pub, as these things so often are – and since then we have researched and portrayed the soldiers of the Régiment de Dillon alongside friends portraying both Jacobite allies and British adversaries. My thanks go out to all who have shared their enthusiasm, their research, and the contents of their libraries over the course of the past ten years and in the preparation of this volume in particular.

Andrew Bamford
Derby, August 2018

# 1

# Backing the Rising

## Politics and Strategy

The connection between France and the Jacobite movement was a long one, going back to the immediate aftermath of the Glorious Revolution of 1688 when James II was driven into exile along with his wife and infant son. The court of Louis XIV provided a home for the royal exile, just as it had for a much younger James four decades previously. This time, though, the presence of the exiled Stuarts in France presented an opportunity which Louis could develop to his advantage in the ongoing European conflict known as the Nine Years War or War of the League of Augsburg. If a counter-invasion of England to restore James to his throne was not an immediate reality, it was possible to open up a new front in Ireland and thus draw off forces from the fighting on the Continent. Defeats at the Boyne, at Aughrim, and at Limerick put paid to Jacobite Ireland, however, and when an invasion of England was eventually assembled the escorting fleet was destroyed by Anglo-Dutch forces at Barfleur and La Hogue in 1692. Thereafter, the aging Louis XIV was pressed by other concerns, and after James II's death in 1701 the likelihood of a French intervention further decreased although Louis was more than happy to recognise the Stuart heir as James III and allow the prince and his mother a continued place at his court.

The situation changed, however, with the death in 1714 of Queen Anne – last of the Protestant Stuarts – and the consequent Hanoverian succession. Coming on top of the 1707 Act of Union, this triggered a new wave of Jacobitisim, particularly focused in Scotland, which led to the Risings of 1715 and 1719. Unfortunately for Jacobite hopes, however, the death of Louis XIV in 1715 meant that French backing for these attempts to restore the Stuarts was simply not forthcoming. Philippe, Duc d'Orléans, Regent for the infant Louis XV, pursued a policy of peace and rapprochement with Britain which culminated in the Anglo-French Treaty of 1716 by which the exiled Stuarts were expelled from France, and this policy continued in a muted form under the regime of Cardinal Fleury, who assumed the role of First Minister after the death of Orléans and the King's majority. Spain, estranged from both Britain and France, supported the '19 alone, but to no avail, and the Anglo-French accord continued throughout the 1720s albeit growing increasingly

'Louis Quinze, Roy de France et de Navarre'; engraving by Petit after Liotard. (Anne S.K. Brown Military Collection)

weak. Only after 1731, when Britain concluded an alliance with Austria, did the balance begin to shift again and relations across the Channel begin to deteriorate. At the same time, a new generation of Stuart princes were growing up in Rome, so that the apparently fading fires of Jacobitsim might yet be fanned back into flame.

Up until the end of the 1730s, therefore, a time had never come to pass when both French and Jacobite attention was focussed on direct action to restore the Stuarts to the British throne by force of arms. When the Jacobites had been most active – in 1689, 1715, and 1719 – France had been distracted at best, allied to the enemy at worst; when France was prepared to make the effort, in 1692, Jacobite fortunes in all three kingdoms were on the wane. As the 1740s opened, however, the advent of a European war and the coming-of-age of James III's heir, Prince Charles Edward Stuart, meant that there was the possibility of an alignment that would aid in the revival of Jacobite fortunes. Matters, however, were by no means clear-cut, with conflicting elements at the French court each pursuing their own agendas in which the Stuart cause variously counted for much, little, or nothing, and with dissent within the Jacobite movement as to how much French aid was necessary for a successful recovery of the British crown, and what form that aid should take. The situation was further complicated by the nature of the hostilities that were spreading across Europe, which, although collectively known to history as the War of the Austrian Succession in fact amounted to a series of interlinked conflicts.

From 1739, Britain and Spain had been engaged in a maritime conflict, the so-called War of Jenkins' Ear, which was focussed on operations in the Americas. Meanwhile, in Europe, the Holy Roman Emperor Carl VI died in 1740 and once he was gone the arrangements that he had made to secure the passage of his inheritance – the Pragmatic Sanction – immediately began to unravel. By its terms, Charles, last male Habsburg in the direct line, was to be succeeded by his daughter Maria Theresa insofar as his own lands were concerned and by her husband, Francis of Lorraine, as Holy Roman Emperor. However, a counter-claim was made by Carl Albrecht, Elector of Bavaria, who was married to the late Emperor's niece. Having already covertly obtained French support for his claim, Carl Albrecht was in due course elected Holy Roman Emperor as Carl VII. Meanwhile, exploiting the confusion, Friedrich II of Prussia – not yet 'the great' but with decided aspirations in that direction and a large and well-drilled army at his disposal – sought to bite off the Habsburg province of Silesia. Maria Theresa thus found herself fighting the Prussians in Silesia (First Silesian War of 1740-1742 and Second Silesian War of 1744-1745), the Bavarians and their French backers in central Europe, and the Spanish and Neapolitans in Italy. Britain, the Dutch Republic, Hanover, Hesse-Cassel, and Piedmont were brought in as allies of the Austrians, ranged against Prussia and the Bourbon powers. The existing Anglo-Spanish war was thus absorbed into the larger conflict, but Britain and France remained very notionally at peace throughout 1743, even though their armies – in the field as auxiliaries to the forces of Maria Theresa and Carl VII respectively – had clashed that year at the Battle of Dettingen.

By 1744, the focus of the war had shifted to the Low Countries. Carl VII had been driven from his Bavarian lands and Prussia showed little inclination to enter the wider war, only re-entering the fighting at all out of opportunism when it seemed that the Habsburg position in Bohemia had been weakened to bolster forces elsewhere. What had begun as a dynastic struggle therefore switched character to become something far more akin to a war of national interest with France seeking to defeat the maritime powers who were her traditional rivals, at the expense of support for her erstwhile Bavarian client, Carl VII, who would in any case die in January 1745. A key weapon in this struggle would be the House of Stuart, and ever since the death of Cardinal Fleury in January 1743 – following which Louis XV had surprised his court by declaring that henceforth he would be his own first minister – active planning had been taking place. This culminated in the covert departure of Charles Edward Stuart from Rome in January 1744 and his subsequent arrival at Dunkirk where he was to form the figurehead of an army which would be shipped across the Channel to restore his father by force of arms.

Charles Edward Stuart, circa 1745. (Anne S.K. Brown Military Collection)

Although largely forgotten by history, since it ultimately came to nought, this proposed invasion was nevertheless a serious and mature scheme. 10,000 men under the command of *Maréchal* Maurice, Comte de Saxe were to embark from Dunkirk and land at Maldon, on the Blackwater Estuary in Essex, from where they would march on London. A further force, three battalions of the French Army's Irish Brigade, would sail for Scotland along with the exiled George Keith, Earl Marischal, a leading light in the '15 and the '19 who was to raise Scotland for the Stuarts. The Irish Brigade at this stage consisted of five single-battalion regiments, and it is not clear which three were earmarked to go to Scotland. As is outlined in the next chapter, 1744 saw the Brigade augmented by an additional Irish regiment and by a Scottish regiment – the Royal Ecossois – which was brigaded with the Irish infantry once it took to the field.

Unfortunately, a plan which relied on calm weather in the waters around the British Isles during winter was always going to place its outcome in the lap of the gods. The French Brest Fleet under *Lieutenant-Général* Jacques Aymar, Comte de Roquefeuil, sailed on 6 February (NS) with 14 sail of the line plus smaller ships, but British intelligence sources were already aware of the mooted operation and Admiral of the Fleet Sir John Norris' fleet of 19 sail of the line was positioned in the Downs – the sheltered waters off the east Kent coast – to block the French movements. Roquefeuil, finding Spithead empty, assumed that he had a clear run up-Channel, and sent word for Saxe to begin his embarkation whilst sending three sail of the line and one smaller ship to escort the transports. Having had other ships detach due to weather damage, he was therefore at a definite disadvantage when he ran into Norris' superior force off Dungeness on 3 March (NS). Roquefeuil sought to escape, and was able to do so thanks to the heavy weather; however, the storm that enabled the Brest Fleet to break contact grew to such a strength that the ships were completely scattered with many of them incurring substantial damage; the 78-year-old Roquefeuil died at sea aboard his flagship before he could return to France.

With the invasion transports also battered by the storm and no chance of getting Saxe's troops across in the face of Norris' fleet, the operation was abandoned. The only possible consolation was that had Saxe and Prince Charles been able to embark and sail when Roquefeuil requested that they do so, the chances are that the Stuart heir, France's best general, and a sizeable proportion of the 10,000 troops would have ended up either in British captivity or at the bottom of the Channel. The composition of Roquefeuil's fleet and Saxe's army are outlined in Tables 1 and 2; it will be noted that, contrary to what has been asserted elsewhere, none of the French ships were actually lost in the operation although several incurred severe weather damage.

'Tencin, Cardinal Archeveque de Lyon, Ministre d'Etat 1758'. (The New York Public Library Digital Collections)

In the aftermath of this disaster, even the Jacobite leadership was split. Charles remained as keen as ever to push forward with some form of rising, but older heads – notably the Earl Marischal – believed that nothing could be done for present. France's policy-makers were equally divided, with three main bodies of opinion forming within the Council of State. Some confidence could be had in the fact that some leading minsters remained openly pro-Jacobite and were willing to support Prince Charles in any further schemes that he might put forward; the lead figures in this group were Cardinal Tencin and the Marquis d'Argenson. Tencin had been tipped to succeed Fleury but was instead brought onto the council without portfolio when Louis XV elected to become his own first minister. Previously a trusted advisor to James III, to whom he owed his cardinal's hat, Tencin was an unswerving supporter of the Stuarts. Tencin initially had the support of the

**Table 1: Roquefeuil's Fleet in February-March 1744**

| Name | Rating | Notes |
|---|---|---|
| *Superbe* | 74 | Flag of *Lieutenant-Général* Comte de Roquefeuil |
| *Dauphin Royal* | 74 | Flag of *Chef d'Escadron* Jean-André de Barrailh; detached to Dunkirk 1 March to cover invasion force |
| *Juste* | 74 | Damaged in collision leaving Brest; re-joined fleet 15 February |
| *Neptune* | 74 | Flag of *Chef d'Escadron* Pierre Blouet de Camilly |
| *Lys* | 72 | |
| *Éclatant* | 64 | |
| *Elisabeth* | 64 | |
| *Fleuron* | 64 | |
| *Mars* | 64 | Detached to Dunkirk 1 March to cover invasion force |
| *Saint Louis* | 64 | |
| *Saint Michel* | 64 | Detached to Brest 19 February due to storm damage |
| *Content* | 60 | Detached to Dunkirk 1 March to cover invasion force |
| *Mercure* | 60 | |
| *Triton* | 60 | Detached to Brest 16 February with sprung mainmast |
| *Apollon* | 56 | |
| *Rubis* | 54 | Joined at sea from Rochefort, 27 February |
| *Argonaute* | 46 | Detached to Dunkirk 1 March to cover invasion force |
| *Parfaite* | 46 | Separated from fleet 14-29 February |
| *Gloire* | 44 | |
| *Vénus* | 26 | Sent into Dunkirk with dispatches, arriving 29 February |
| *Médée* | 26 | Dismasted 1 March and made for French coast |
| *Subtile* | 26 | |
| *Dryade* | 12 | Detached to Brest for repairs 19 February |

All dates in table are New Style. Those ships marked as detached to Dunkirk did not return in time for the meeting of the fleets of Dungeness. For comparison, Norris' fleet consisted of one ship of 100 guns, four of 90, three of 80, three of 70, one of 64, and seven of 60, plus 12 smaller warships. Ship details from *Three Decks – Warships in the Age of Sail*, at www.threedecks.org, supplemented by additional information provided by Albert Parker from his forthcoming work on naval operations in the War of the Austrian Succession.

Marquis d'Argenson, who replaced Jean-Jacques Amelot at the foreign affairs portfolio after the latter was disgraced following the failure of the invasion scheme, which he had championed. Outside of the Council of State, Tencin could also count upon the support of leading military figures *Maréchal* Charles Louis August Fouquet, Duc de Belle-Isle, and *Lieutenant Général* Armand de Vignerot du Plessis, Duc de Richelieu.

Directly opposed to this bloc and unwilling to expend any further energy to advance the Stuart cause were *Maréchal* Adrien, Duc de Noailles, and the Comptroller-General (finance minister) Philibert Orry de Fulvy. Noailles was close to Louis and the King's most influential military advisor, although his star had dipped since Dettingen where he had been in chief command but had allowed his nephew and protégé the Duc de Gramont to make the fatal blunder that cost the battle. He favoured limited war aims, peace between Britain and France, a break with Prussia as a means of reconciling with the

Table 2: Troops Assembled at Dunkirk for the Invasion of England, January 1744

| Units | Battalions | Officers | Men |
|---|---|---|---|
| Régiment de Monaco | 3 | 77 | 1,783 |
| Régiment de Gondrin | 2 | 35 | 1,130 |
| Régiment de Eu | 2 | 23 | 960 |
| Régiment Royal la Marine | 1 | 13 | 522 |
| Régiment de Languedoc | 1 | 14 | 615 |
| Régiment de La Cour au Chantre (Swiss) | 2 | 27 | 1,146 |
| Régiment de Soissonais | 1 | 25 | 581 |
| Régiment de Bauffrement | 1 | 17 | 552 |
| Régiment de Diesbach (Swiss) | 2 | 30 | 1,198 |
| Régiment Royal Corse | 1 | 33 | 493 |
| Régiment de Dragons de Dauphin | - | 27 | 595 |
| Cannoniers de la Marine | - | 13 | 120 |
| **Totals** | **16** | **334** | **9,695** |

The Régiments de Languedoc, de Diesbach, and Royal Corse replaced the Régiment de Navarre, originally assigned to the expedition. Saxe was to be seconded by *Lieutenants-Généraux* Lutteaux and du Chayla and *Maréchaux de Camp* Berranger, d'Apcher, Langeron, and Rambures, and a full staff was provided including engineer and medical personnel along with a ten-man detachment of military police to keep the rest in order. Information from J. Colin, *Louis XV et Les Jacobites: Le Projet de Débarquement en Angleterre de 1743-1744* (Paris: Librarie Militaire de R. Chapelot & Cie, 1901), pp.77-81.

'Adrien Maurice Duc de Noailles Pair et Maréchal de France, &c'. (The New York Public Library Digital Collections)

Habsburgs, and an end to over-ambitious schemes such as the 1744 invasion attempt, which he had opposed. For Orry, who had had charge of France's accounts since 1730, his reason for providing no further aid to the Stuarts was simply financial; such quixotic gestures did not aid in balancing the books.

The final pair were those whose attitude was pragmatic, as befit the ministers responsible for coordinating France's war effort; these were the Comte d'Argenson, younger brother of the new Foreign Minister, who held the post of Secretary of State for War, and his naval counterpart, Jean Fréderic Phélpeaux, Comte de Maurepas, Minister of Marine. Both men were at odds with Orry, whose peacetime parsimony had weakened France's armed forces, and Maurepas was an arch-enemy of Tencin and of the Duc de Richelieu. Thus, while there was little to connect them to the pro-Stuart faction both men were willing to dabble in further Jacobite adventures if it furthered their own aims. For the Comte d'Argenson, these were simply to continue the war so that he could continue to enjoy the power and prestige of a wartime Secretary of State for War; his ambitions were for personal glory and the titles that might come with it. Maurepas, on the other hand, was a more complex character with wider ambitions. The Ministry of Marine was responsible not just for the navy but for France's colonies, where

Maurepas saw scope for large-scale expansion; in particular, he sought to use the outbreak of war with Britain as an opportunity to recapture Newfoundland which had been ceded under the 1713 Treaty of Utrecht. This operation, however, and the greater colonial expansion that was to follow it, could only be achieved by breaking the Royal Navy's control of the seas and so any means of striking against Britain was to be pursued. Such means therefore included assisting the Stuarts in their plots even though Muarepas openly expressed his doubts about the existence of English Jacobites in any number and of the ability of French naval forces to support even a Scottish-based rising.

'Le Comte d'Argenson'. (The New York Public Library Digital Collections)

In effect, Maurepas and the Comte d'Argenson held the balance of power in the Council of State. Guaranteed the support of the pro-Stuart faction when an opportunity arose of which they were in favour, but also able to ally with the anti-Stuart faction to squash French involvement in any Jacobite adventuring that they perceived as unwise or unhelpful to the French cause, they helped to ensure that France's contribution to the Rising of 1745 was initially discrete, always limited, and ultimately intended to advance French policy with the minimum of actual effort and expenditure.

## Private Enterprise

In the aftermath of the failed invasion scheme, the anti-Stuart faction held sway. The Armée de Flandres, commanded by Noailles and accompanied by Louis in person, took the field in the Low Countries and made good initial progress before a Habsburg offensive forced a redeployment to the Rhine. The King then fell gravely ill at Metz, to the point that his life was despaired of: this removed a further plank of potential support for the Stuarts as Louis, at least when in his pious moods, had loosely favoured the idea of aiding in the re-establishment of the Catholic dynasty as a means of atoning for his own not-inconsiderable sins of the flesh. After his recovery, Louis continued to pursue a broadly pro-Stuart line but deferred to his ministers on the matter and, in any case, continued to take a personal interest in military affairs on the Continent. The following year, the focus of war shifted back to Flanders with French forces, now under Saxe but with Noailles and the King still in the field, winning a great victory at Fontenoy on 11 May 1745 (NS) over the Anglo-Dutch under the Duke of Cumberland. This further committed France to an extended campaign in the Low Countries as Saxe moved to exploit his victory.

The result of all this was that Charles began to think increasingly on the idea of going it alone so far as an initial landing in Scotland was concerned, in the hope that this would force the French hand and oblige them to send him further aid. He was confident that, at the least, he would be thereby able to secure the services of the Irish troops in French service. To even get to Scotland, however, would require some outside help and the whole concept of such a venture risked compromising many loyal Scottish and English Jacobites if it ended in disaster; Charles' father therefore counselled against anything rash on the latter grounds. The Earl Marischal, meanwhile, was wary of anything that would see Charles, and thus the Jacobite cause as a whole, cynically deployed in any scheme that would nominally assist their cause but which would in reality make them the dupes of just the sort of self-interested French gambit that Maurepas and the Comte d'Argenson now envisaged. Charles, however, chose to ignore both sets of advice and to continue with his plans.

The thing that got things moving for the young prince was the existence of a flourishing Franco-Irish mercantile community working out of the ports of western France. By no means had all of the Irish families who followed James II into exile stuck purely to the sword, and branches of many of the same dynasties who provided the leaders of the Irish Brigade also had their interests in ship owning, in the West Indian trade and, come wartime, in privateering. These men were Jacobites of a sort, it is true, but they were primarily businessmen and, as the historian Bruce Lenman suggests, stood greatly to gain in their privateering endeavours if Britain were in turmoil and the Royal Navy distracted: a common ground between these men and Maurepas is obvious.[1]

Through connections with this body, Charles was able to secure the services of one Antoine Walsh and his ship *La Doutelle*, a small frigate of 16 guns, to carry him and a small party to Scotland. However, space for both cargo and men aboard so small a ship was limited, and her handful of light guns, though ample for a privateer, would avail her little if she ran into a Royal Navy warship. She needed an escort and in this the Prince was obliged by another Franco-Irishman, Sir Walter Ruttledge, who was able to secure the loan from the French navy of an out-of-commission warship, the *Elisabeth* of 64 guns, permission for which was given by Maurepas. Ostensibly, the reason for the loan of the ship – which was, in itself, by no means irregular although it was less usual for so large a warship to be employed on private service – was to facilitate a privateering expedition to the West Indies, although it was suspected even at the time that the Minister really knew exactly what Ruttledge and his confederates wanted the ship for.

Not only would the *Elisabeth* provide an escort for the Prince in *La Doutelle*, she would also carry arms and equipment for the army that he hoped to raise and, indeed, a nucleus for that army. However, the nature of the ship and her cargo have become somewhat obscured and it is as well to review them and establish exactly what was being provided to the Jacobites. Firstly, the ship herself was not, as is often asserted, the 70-gun ship of that name captured from the Royal Navy in 1704; that vessel, although taken into the French service as a prize, was broken up in 1720. The ship with which

---

1    Bruce Lenman, *The Jacobite Risings in Britain 1689-1746* (Aberdeen: Scottish Cultural Press, 1995), pp.241-241.

we are interested was laid down at Brest in 1722, launched the same year, and first commissioned two years after that. She was of 950 tons burthen and, as built, was armed with 24 24-pounders on the lower gun-deck, 26 12-pounders on the upper, and 14 6-pounders on her upperworks. This gave her a rated total of 64 guns but it is possible that she was carrying fewer pieces than this when she sailed for Scotland as some accounts refer to her as a ship of 60 guns. She had formed part of Roquefeuil's ill-fated fleet but had survived the storm and, by the summer of 1745,was repaired and refitted under the command of *Capitaine* d'O (also given as Dau – the exact identity of this officer is not clear).[2]

That much, then, is clear enough. When we get onto the subject of the men who were on board then the situation becomes rather complicated, although, in fact it should not because we have the Prince's own record which quite clearly stated to his father that there were '700 men aboured [sic] as also a company of sixty Volontiers [sic] all gentlemen'.[3] This seems fairly straightforward: 700 men as the ship's company – which is perhaps a little on the high side for a relatively small two-decker although Charles was here reporting second-hand information – and 60 soldiers. Unfortunately, some accounts have translated '700 men' into 700 soldiers, and further complicated matters by assuming, apparently because Charles had been introduced to Walsh, Ruttledge, and their confederates by Charles O'Brien, 6th Viscount Clare, who was a *lieutenant général* in the French service and colonel of the eponymous Irish regiment, that these troops came from the Régiment de Clare. All of this is simply unreasonable; 700 troops could not have viably been embarked along with a crew and other cargo unless a substantial portion of the *Elisabeth*'s guns were taken out, which they were not. Furthermore, the Régiment de Clare had in total at this time a total all-ranks strength of 495 and so even if the entire unit had been sent down from Flanders to the Biscay coast, which it was not and which would only have been possible with the sort of official sanction which the Jacobites and their confederates did not possess, it would still not have been enough to make up the assumed quota of troops.[4]

This does, however, raise the question of who the troops on board the *Elisabeth* actually were. The answer is no more or less than that provided by Charles himself, namely that they were a body of volunteers apparently recruited for the putative West Indian privateering operation; indeed, they were even named the Compagnie de Maurepas after the sponsoring Minister. For an account of them we have the intelligence provided by the Dutch ambassador at the French court, Abraham van Hoey, as conveyed to John Hay, 4th Marquess of Tweeddale, Secretary of State for Scotland:

---

2   Ship data from *Three Decks – Warships in the Age of Sail*, at www.threedecks.org.
3   Quoted in Jacqueline Riding, *Jacobites. A New History of the '45 Rebellion* (London: Bloomsbury, 2016), p.64.
4   Unit strength of 1 June (NS) 1745 from J. Colin, *Les Campagnes de Maréchal de Saxe* (Paris: Librarie Militaire de R. Chapelot & Cie, 1906), Vol.III, p.482.

They say he had 70 noblemen in uniform to protect him and 300 volunteers, some of whom had been recruited in this town. This troop is dressed in blue, rather like Hussars, with a tiny golden braid on the jacket, hats trimmed with gold and red plumes, and sabres. I have seen many of that sort here.[5]

Van Hoey's account is useful for a number of reasons not least because it helps reconcile Charles' account of 60 gentlemen volunteers with his surprisingly-large figure of 700 crew for the *Elisabeth*. If, per Van Hoey's version – and we need to make some allowance here for the 'they say' element; clearly this was not all first-hand knowledge – 300 of that 700 were troops then that leaves a more realistic 400 crewmen which is in accordance with the 400-450 men given as the established compliment for the *Elisabeth* when in regular naval service.

Additionally, though, van Hoey's description is the best one that we have of the uniform of these men and allows a reconstruction of it to be made. In aiding this, a further clue is given by the fact that a number of accounts, going back to James Ray's contemporary history, refer to these troops as 'Grassins de Mer'. This raises a comparison with the famous Légion de Grassin, an all-arms corps of light troops raised in 1744 by the Comte de Grassin and distinguished at Fontenoy. Grassin's men, infantry as well as cavalry, adopted hussar-style uniform including tall mirliton caps and the implication, therefore, is that the men of the Compagnie de Maurepas also wore these rather than the usual cocked hats. This assumption is given further credence by the fact that van Hoey notes that these men wore plumes, something not normally seen with cocked hats but a typical adornment of a mirliton. The adoption of such an exotic uniform was not without sense or precedent. For troops raised – however notionally – to act as marines on a privateering expedition, short coats make more sense aboard ship than full length frock coats, whilst in respect of their actual intended role of impressing the locals once Charles arrived in Scotland the result would certainly have looked striking. As for precedent, the fame of the Légion de Grassin after Fontenoy meant that its distinctive uniform was aped by other new units raised on the same model; the dress of the Volontaires Bretons, raised in 1746, for example, was almost identical to that described by van Hoey for the Compagnie de Maurepas bar for the employment of buff rather than red as a facing colour.

As for the weapons and stores embarked, these were all provided by the Ministry of Marine but, again, as with the troops, plausible deniability was maintained by the fiction that they were all intended for the privateering expedition. It does make one wonder, however, just who was fooled by this cover story; if even the Dutch ambassador was aware of what the troops were really intended for then it is stretching the bounds of probability to believe that the Minister of Marine did not know what was afoot. The suspicion,

---

5   Copy of Intelligence sent from van Hoey to Tweedale, National Archives of Scotland, GD1/609/4/4c: in the original: '*Il a, dit on 70 Gardes pour Gentelshommes habillés en uniformes, et 300 Volontaires d'ont partie ont ête levés en cette Ville. Cette troupe est habillée en Bleu, à peu pres comme Hussars, avec un petit Tresse d'or sur l'habit et des Chapeaux border d'Or avec des plummets rouges, et des Sabres, j'en ai vue plusieurs de cette Espece ici*'.

therefore, is that Maurepas deliberately ensured that Charles was given just enough aid to get him to Scotland – just enough rope to hang himself with – with the Minister confident that, win or lose, the Stuart Prince would divert the British from their war effort long enough to create a window of opportunity on which France could capitalise.

As luck would have it, the men of the Compagnie de Maurepas never got the chance to impress the inhabitants of the Highlands with their braided uniforms and fancy hats. On 14 July (NS) *La Doutelle* sailed from Nantes and the following day she made rendezvous with the *Elisabeth*. Off the Lizard on 20 July (NS – 9 July OS), however, the little flotilla ran into a British warship, the 58-gun *Lion*. Although carrying fewer guns than the *Elisabeth* the British ship was larger and in better condition, and after an evenly-matched fight the two warships pounded each other without either side being able to obtain the advantage. Every officer aboard the *Lion* was wounded, and *Capitaine* d'O of the *Elisabeth* killed. Eventually the two ships broke off the fight for the simple reason that neither was in a fit state to continue it, leaving the Prince to continue to Scotland with only the men and resources available aboard *La Doutelle*.

There is neither the space nor the scope within this book to examine the Prince's campaign in any detail. It is useful, however, to explore the role of French professionals in its early stages up to the retreat from Derby back to Scotland at which juncture Charles was joined by the French regular troops whose composition and activities form the main part of this study.

Of Charles' companions when he landed from *La Doutelle* – the so-called 'Seven Men of Moidart', although that figure ignores the presence of various servants and other 'extras' – two were officers of the French army: Sir John MacDonald, *colonel* of the mounted component of the Irish contingent in the French service, the Régiment de Fitzjames, and John William O'Sullivan. O'Sullivan was also Irish by ancestry but possessed of a French commission and formerly a *capitaine* on the staff of the Marquis de Mallebois during that officer's conquest of Corsica, and later in Italy and on the Rhine. MacDonald, aging and apparently fond of the bottle, would play only a minor role in events to come as Inspector of Cavalry in the Jacobite army, but O'Sullivan, who was made a colonel by Charles, would play a pivotal role as its Quartermaster-General and de facto chief-of-staff. O'Sullivan had acted in a very similar capacity under Mallebois, something which he must have done to a reasonable degree of satisfaction since his master was in 1741 accorded the dignity of *Maréchal*. The fact that the campaign on Corsica was in essence one of irregulars versus regulars must also have given O'Sullivan some insight into the situation faced by the Jacobites in 1745, albeit that on Corsica he had been on the regular side of things rather than the reverse.

In the initial stages of the campaign, as Charles built up an army on the march and on the fly, O'Sullivan exercised more of a command role, including the direction of the initial abortive attempt to capture Ruthven Barracks. Here, his attempts to instil some military realism into the situation clashed, not for the last time, with the Jacobite desire for immediate action. Thus, notwithstanding a lack of the artillery judged necessary to reduce such a strongpoint, an attack was made and repulsed, much to the credit of the tiny garrison. There would be similar differences of opinion in the manoeuvring that took place before the Battle of Prestonpans, with Lord George Murray – lieutenant general and, in his own mind at least, the military brains of the Jacobite army – advocating immediate action whilst O'Sullivan called a delay until the moment was right. The fact that O'Sullivan again had the right of things doubtless did not help matters, and the result was a polarisation of opinions with contemporaries then, and historians ever since, split between the two perspectives.

The idea that the Jacobite army of the '45 was a modern military force has been expanded upon at some length by Christopher Duffy in his work on the Rising, albeit that the differences between the Jacobite organisation and typical Continental practice have been exaggerated to the detriment of the former. In reality, the Jacobite organisation was not more advanced than that employed elsewhere in Europe, but differed primarily in that its organisation was tailored to suit its composition. The employment of distinct Highland and Lowland Divisions during the English campaign, something which was retained afterwards but in a less distinct form, made the most of the capabilities of the fast-marching Highland troops whilst still retaining a useful role for the Lowlanders. Jacobite cavalry could not operate on the battlefield, but functioned excellently as a scouting and screening force. This sort of professionalism could not have been developed so quickly, maybe even at all, without the experience of O'Sullivan and other officers with experience of Continental army organisation and staff work in particular. Indeed, the specifically French influence is subtly present in the Jacobite army's daily orders where the terminology drawn upon – the establishment of picquets; soldiers referred to as fusiliers; on at least one occasion the use of the French term 'Aide Majors' where adjutants is meant – is clearly taken from the norms that O'Sullivan would have been used to whilst serving on Mallebois' staff.[6] This was all very efficient, although Lord George Murray felt that O'Sullivan left too much unsaid and that the Jacobites, being amateur soldiers, needed to have things spelled out to them in more detail.

By the time that the Jacobite army struck south-west from Edinburgh to Carlisle and then on into England, O'Sullivan and MacDonald had been joined by more French officers and by an envoy of Louis XV, the Marquis d'Eguilles, of whom more anon. Murray sniffed that these officers' military knowledge was so lacking that they were barely able to mount guard effectively – which is a little rich, from someone whose only professional military experience was as a subaltern in Marlborough's day – but whilst some may well have been adventurers others proved themselves competent and effective officers. Richard Warren, for example, a bankrupt merchant from Marseilles who had previously served as a volunteer with the French army and had attached himself to Eguilles' suite, was perhaps the best example of the first category, certainly possessed of little prior military knowledge, although this did

---

6    Brevet-Colonel Sir Bruce Seton (ed.), *The Orderly Book of Lord Ogilvie's Regiment in the Army of Prince Charles Edward Stuart 10 October, 1745, to 21 April, 1746* (Heaton Mersey: The Cloister Press for the Society of Army Historical Research, 1923); see in particular orders for 7-8 March 1746, p.47, for the employment of 'Aide Majors'.

not stop him organising the crossing of the Dornoch Firth in March 1746, which Duffy accounts 'the prettiest operation of the '45'.[7] At the other end of the scale were the veteran professionals John Bagot and James Grant, who respectively revitalised the Jacobite hussars and artillery.

John – or Jean – Bagot was a long-service veteran who provided the leadership that turned the Jacobite hussars from a rabble into an effective light cavalry force that has gone down in history under his name. Interestingly, Bagot was not a cavalryman by prior service. Born in 1695 at Saint-Germain-en-Laye, then home to the Jacobite court in exile, he was commissioned at the age of 12 into what was then the Régiment de Dorrington (later Rooth) and by 1745 was *major* and a chevalier of the *Ordre de Saint Louis*. What was required in his new role – which made him a Jacobite colonel – was not the skills of a particular arm of service, however, but the firm leadership and experience that came from over three decades of constant service, and that is exactly what he brought.[8] In a similar fashion, James Grant was yet another infantryman, this time of the Régiment de Lally, but he was evidently possessed of a full military education for his conduct of the Jacobite artillery train, and of such of the sieges as he was engaged in, was consistently professional and competent even allowing for the limited tools with which he had to work. Like Bagot, Grant was made a colonel in the Jacobite service.

Other French officers, as we shall see, would similarly be drafted into command positions in Jacobite units as the Rising progressed, but the particular employment of Franco-Irish officers proved to be contentious and revealed a Jacobite necessity to balance military and political needs, as well as the importance of representing the foreign support for the Stuart cause in the best possible light. Charles had high hopes that recruits would flock to his standard from the ranks of the English Jacobites, and to that end had pre-planned the establishment of English regiments for his army with two Franco-Irish officers, Sir Francis Geohegan and Ignatious Browne, given commissions to raise such units (it is for this reason that Browne, though a *capitaine* in the Régiment de Lally, is 'Colonel Browne' in many accounts). This proposal, however, was met with some level of protest from the Scots Episcopalian element, which objected to the appointment of two Catholic officers, and its wisdom was questioned more generally with respect to the potential negative publicity inherent in giving high appointments to Catholic officers of a foreign power. The result was that the colonelcy of what became the Jacobite Manchester Regiment went instead to Francis Towneley, of Towneley Hall, Burnley, who, whilst Catholic, was at least an Englishman. Towneley, however, was also the holder of a French commission, having served for some years in the Régiment de Limousin and, more recently, had been earmarked for a colonelcy ahead of the abortive 1744 invasion attempt. Having served actively during the War of the Polish Succession, including at the Siege of Philippsburg, Towneley was able to bring a not-inconsiderable

---

7   Christopher Duffy, *Fight for a Throne. The Jacobite '45 Reconsidered* (Solihull: Helion, 2015), p.319
8   Major A. McK. Annand, 'The Hussars of the '45', *JSAHR*, Vol.XXXIX, No.159 (September 1961), pp.144-160; see in particular pp.158-159 for Bagot's service history.

The south-west prospect of the city of Carlisle; hand coloured engraving by and after Samuel and Nathaniel Buck. (Anne S.K. Brown Military Collection)

amount of military experience to the post, probably at the very least on a par with that of the two Irish *capitaines*.

Browne and Geohegan nevertheless remained with the Jacobite army during the English campaign, but were left behind as part of the garrison left to hold Carlisle Castle along with another French officer, *Capitaine* Sir John Arbuthnot of the Royal Ecossois. Francis Strickland, an English Jacobite of a Westmoreland family and another of the Seven Men of Moidart, is also listed amongst the French officers in the list of prisoners taken when the castle fell, but if he had held a French commission in the past he was certainly not an active officer in the French service during the '45. There were also a number of stray French rank-and-file, enumerated as one *sergent* and four soldiers of the Régiment de Lally.[9] It is not clear what purpose these latter were meant to serve. One or two private soldiers can be explained away as the servants of the officers, but the inclusion of an NCO hints at some larger purpose – perhaps a recruiting party. The names of the rank and file prisoners are given as *Sergent* Pierre la Locke and *Fusiliers* Pierre Bourgogne, Francis Carpentier, Jean Poussin, and Pierre Vickman: these are not representative Irish names, a point which will be addressed in detail in the next chapter.[10]

Arbuthnot and Geohegan both went into captivity with the garrison, as did Towneley and the bulk of his regiment, but Browne took the opportunity to make his escape over the wall in the company of a Scots officer during the confusion after the castle was surrendered. Arbuthnot and Geohegan were both treated as regular prisoners of war, but Towneley eventually went to the block. Although his defence used his French commission as a plea when he came to trial, the fact that he had left the British Isles to serve a foreign power without obtaining permission to do so was deemed to have stripped this defence of any validity; to this must be added the fact that he was not serving as a French officer either prior to or during the Rising, and, on a more practical if less legally-sound principle, to the desire to make a gory example of the handful of English Jacobites taken in arms.

9    Andrew Henderson, *The History of the Rebellion of MDCCXLV and MDCCXLVI* (London: A. Millar, 1753), p.202.

10   Names as reported in the *Newcastle Courant*, quoted in Stuart Reid, *1745. A Military History of the Last Jacobite Rising* (Staplehurst: Spellmount, 1996), p.91.

The fact that the all-ranks strength of the French contingent during the English campaign could be counted on one's fingers, and the fact that so few English Jacobites joined the cause that Towneley's short-lived regiment of English Jacobites never had more than 250 or so men on its strength, are not unconnected. From the outset, Charles' supporters in both Scotland and England had urged that nothing be attempted without significant French support; the young Prince's enthusiasm had carried the day in Scotland against older and wiser judgements, but the English Jacobites wanted to see a French invasion before they showed their hands and it was clear that none was forthcoming. The same lack was a key reason given by the Highland officers for the decision to turn back at Derby in December 1745 rather than press on for London. This, then, begs the question of how the French authorities did respond to the Rising, and the nature and extent of the aid and support that they were able to send.

## Fait Acompli

Although some update on the progress of Charles' expedition was available upon the return to France of the battered *Elisabeth* after the sea-fight off the Lizard, it was not until Walsh and *La Doutelle* returned from Scotland that it was known for certain that Charles was ashore and that the rising was underway. Louis XV and his ministers were therefore presented with a *fait acompli*, albeit one about which they had almost certainly known was likely; what they now had to do was decide how best to take advantage of it.

One option, perhaps the most cynical of all, was simply to do nothing and make the most of things on the Continent as British troops were withdrawn – which they surely would be, if the Rising were to be contained. Such a withdrawal would leave Austria over-stretched and Hanover vulnerable to Prussia, and open up opportunities for France in the Low Countries where Saxe's army had continued to advance after its victory at Fontenoy. Alternatively, the Marquis d'Argenson, wavering for the moment from his usually pro-Jacobite stance, saw the opportunity to bring about a negotiated peace that would enable Britain to free herself from her Continental entanglements – to French advantage, naturally – in order to deal with the Stuarts: this line ultimately came to nothing, not least as George II was able to come to an understanding with Friedrich II, beginning a British rapprochement with Prussia but at the price of accepting Prussian control over Silesia.

The general French consensus was one of wait-and-see, although this did mean fending off Jacobite demands – made initially by the Earl Marischal and Lord Clancarty – for 10,000 men and the arms for another 30,000. Perhaps realising that he had been too ambitious, Marischal made a second request, directly to the King, for 4,000 troops which he would personally lead to Scotland; Louis was sympathetic, but threw the proposal over to Maurepas and the Comte d'Argenson, who were able to kill it off for the time being. Maurepas, indeed, had even less time for the Stuart cause than normal at this point, being primarily concerned at this time with the loss of France's fortress of Louisburg, on Cape Breton, which had fallen to an expedition mounted from Britain's New England colonies and whose capture further dented his grand colonial plans.

After further royal prodding, the Minister of Marine did eventually produce a memorandum on the practicalities of sending aid to the Jacobites. In it, he demolished the arguments for sending reinforcements to Scotland by sea, citing the distance, the fact that the Royal Navy would be on the alert, and France's near-crippling lack of shipping and sailors. Large transports would need to be well-victualled for the long voyage, and this would cut down on their carrying capacity. The costs would vastly outweigh even the 900,000 livres expended on the abortive 1744 invasion. Recognising, however, that Louis clearly wanted to see something done, Maurepas proposed an extension of the private enterprise scheme that had got Charles to Scotland in the first place. Although the Biscay ports had the capacity for sending up to 4,000 troops to the west coast of Scotland by this means, the preferred option would be fast ships operating out of Dunkirk and recently-captured Ostend and running up to the east coast ports. The only other serious proposal sent in came from *Maréchal* de Noailles, who proposed a French landing in Ireland as a further distraction which could be mounted at minimum risk using France's own Irish troops as a nucleus and which would save France becoming directly involved on the British mainland at all.

Whilst Louis was mulling over the options, he had, as noted, sent an envoy to make contact with the Jacobites in the shape of Alexandre Jean Baptiste de Boyer, Marquis d'Eguilles. A devout and somewhat old-fashioned individual, and holding a commission as *capitaine* in the *Compagnies Franches de la Marine*, France's naval/colonial infantry corps, Eguilles was appointed by the Marquis d'Argenson and considered to be the 'creature' of Tencin, thus making him eminently suitable to work with the Jacobites but, perhaps also, a little too ready to bend to their way of thinking.[11] Sailing aboard the Dunkirk privateer *l'Espérance*, he disembarked at Montrose and waited upon Charles at Holyrood House, where the Prince had established his court following the fall of Edinburgh and the victory at Prestonpans, on 14. Eguilles was immediately acclaimed by the Jacobites as the French Ambassador, something which he was not (although Louis would later raise him to that status). The ships which followed the envoy during the next few days brought arms and funding for the Jacobites, including cannon and, as we have seen, the handful of French officers and troops who participated in the English campaign and ended up at Carlisle. Eguilles would remain with Charles for the remainder of the Rising, where his advice during the English campaign that French help was already on the way and that an invasion was imminent – whilst perhaps reflecting the aspirations of his political backers – was, to say the least, wishful thinking.

This is not to say, however, that an invasion was not seriously mooted, but the very speed of the Jacobite advance into England caught the French

---

11  Eguilles' commission in the *Compagnies Franches de la Marine* is confirmed by the listing in 'An Etat of the French Officers Prisoners of War att Penrith Ye 11th November 1746', TNA, SP36/89, pp.115-6.

very much on the hop. It was one thing to run small bodies of men up from Dunkirk to Scotland, and news of the Jacobite victory at Prestonpans and the success of Eguilles' mission accelerated preparations for this, but an invasion force of 10,000 men could not simply be strung together out of nothing.

On 24 October (NS) the secret Treaty of Fontainebleau was signed by the Marquis d'Argenson on behalf of Louis XV and Daniel O'Brien, the Stuart representative at the French court, on behalf of James III. Its terms bound Louis to assist the Jacobites in all possible ways, and granted them the use of the Scots and Irish troops in French service to assist in their endeavours, requiring in return only that the officers of these regiments be permitted to recruit for them whilst in the British Isles. In the short term, it was agreed to send troops to Scotland in the shape of the Régiment Royal Ecossois and a provisional battalion of Irish Picquets formed out of detachments from each of the six Irish infantry regiments in French service. An account of the composition, uniform, equipment, and service of these troops forms the bulk of the rest of this work but it is first as well to review the ongoing plans for the dispatch of further troops, which, although they never brought about the full invasion that the Jacobites were hoping for, did ensure that additional French troops would sail for Scotland – some of them in time to take part in the final battles of the Rising.

'Le Maréchal Richelieu à l'age de 30 ans'. (The New York Public Library Digital Collections)

During November and December, a substantial force of troops was drawn off from France's field armies and assembled at Dunkirk where command was invested in the Duc de Richelieu with Clare as his second. As well as the Irish troops – six battalions of infantry and one regiment of cavalry – there were five French battalions – two apiece from the regiments of Crillon and Orléans and one from the Régiment de Beauvoisis – and one from an unspecified Walloon regiment in French service as well as two 'mixed battalions' under the Duc de Fronsac (son and heir to the Duc de Richelieu) which were presumably made up from men drafted from other units. Later the cavalry regiments of Royal-Etranger, Chabrillant, Clermont-Tonerre, and Maugiron were added to the force along with the dragoons of the Régiment de Septimanie.[12] Antoine Walsh was to oversee the transportation of these troops across the Channel once preparations were complete – hopefully by mid-December – and the younger of the Stuart princes, Henry Benedict, Duke of York was to provide the expedition with a suitable figurehead.

---

12 Listing from F.J. McLynn, *France and the Jacobite Rising of 1745* (Edinburgh: Edinburgh University Press, 1981), pp.115, 157; McLynn, working from contemporary intelligence reports, also lists three battalions of the 'Scots Royal' (but names only two commanders for them); it is not entirely clear what units these are meant to indicate, since the Royal Ecossois had but one battalion and that had already gone to Scotland.

Here, however, was evidence that the over-positive reports of the Jacobite representatives at the French court – every other English nobleman a Jacobite, widespread support for the Stuarts throughout the British isles – was in fact counting against them. Rather than hurrying the preparations to seize the opportunity and capitalise on the Jacobite gamble, the French dawdled and took their time. This was not helped by the Comte d'Argenson's unwillingness to hurry the dispatch of supplies and Orry's parsimonious refusal to advance the necessary funds, which, along with the intrigues of Mme. Pompadour, would cost him his post before the year was out. For the invasion to have affected Charles' English campaign it would need to have been made in the first week of December (OS – mid-December NS) and the reality was that matters were at that point still some weeks from being ready. Thereafter, once the Jacobites had turned back from Derby on 6 December (17 December NS) the raison d'être of the whole operation was lost although preparations still continued. It might reasonably be suggested that the ideal plan would have been for the Jacobites to have consolidated their position in Scotland over the winter of 1745-46 and mounted an invasion of England in the spring in conjunction with a French landing; such a scheme, however, could have required greater coordination between the French and Jacobite leaders than was realistic once Charles was in Scotland, and would have cost the Jacobites valuable momentum. Of course, an attempted landing at any time in 1745 or 1746 would have been opposed by the Royal Navy, whose forces in the Channel under Admiral Edward Vernon were on the guard against that very eventuality. Other issues aside, the strength of the Royal Navy alone casts doubt on whether the operation could ever have stood a chance of success. Indeed, Vernon's smaller warships harried and attacked the transports even as they sought to assemble, further disrupting the plans.

By January, with news of Derby now received and confirmed, it was clear that matters could not proceed, and the operation was shelved. The troop concentration began to break up, until only the Irish troops remained poised for sailing. The cavalrymen of the Régiment de Fitzjames were safely embarked from Ostend, only for three quarters of them to be captured at sea, whilst attempts to get more infantry across either amounted to nothing or else never sailed. At the very end of the Rising, in the spring of 1746, the remaining men of the regiments of Berwick and Clare at Dunkirk, Rooth at Ostend, and Bulkeley, Dillon, and Lally at Boulogne, were prepared to go over entire, and elements of the first pair actually sailed and reached the coast of Scotland but did not land. Only a small detachment of the Régiment de Berwick would actually land in Scotland as a final pre-Culloden reinforcement for the Irish Picquets. For France, though, even the threat of invasion had been to her advantage; a further distraction for the Royal Navy just as Maurepas had intended. It is doubtful whether he, or the Comte d'Argenson, had ever seriously intended that the invasion should go ahead. Maurepas' priority at this time was building up the Brest Fleet in order to retake Louisbourg and perhaps fulfil his long-held hope of regaining Newfoundland whilst his counterpart at the Ministry of War was happy to hold troops in readiness along the Channel during the winter so long as they could join Saxe when the French armies took the field again in the spring. Saxe, indeed, was one of the greatest beneficiaries of the '45, winning another great victory at Rocoux on 1 October 1746 (NS) against a largely Austro-Dutch allied army that included only a couple of brigades of British troops, the rump of an army left behind in Flanders while the rest returned to Britain. Nevertheless, French troops would fight just as hard in Scotland as they did in Flanders, and it is to the story of those troops that we must now turn.

2

# Regiments and Soldiers

## Lineage and Organisation

The Irish Brigade – which, as we have seen, also included the Royal Ecossois – has become one of the most famed formations in French military history, at least so far as the English-speaking world is concerned. It therefore comes as something of a surprise to learn that their reputation in contemporary French circles was less than stellar, and that their selection of men from the units of the brigade to go to Scotland seems to have been down to their obvious Jacobite credentials and their expendability rather than their military prowess. Furthermore, when the composition of these units is addressed in detail it becomes clear that they were by no means as uniformly 'Irlandois' or 'Ecoissois' as their regimental titles might suggest. This chapter explores these contradictions, to provide a better picture of the officers and men who served in Scotland.

The origins of the Irish Brigade go back to 1690, when James II was fighting for his crown in Ireland having been driven from England in the 'Glorious Revolution' of 1688. Much of the largely Catholic Irish population had rallied to his cause but the British Army had gone over to the new regime of William and Mary, and enthusiastic but untrained Jacobite volunteers required supplementing by veteran regular troops. James accordingly struck a deal with Louis XIV of France: James would send Louis a brigade of Irish troops to join the French army, which was fighting the English, Austrians, and Dutch in Europe, in return for which Louis would – eventually – send French regulars to help James in Ireland. The brigade sent to France was commanded by Viscount Mountcashel, and was organised for the French service into three regiments, whose colonels were Mountcashel himself, the Hon. Daniel O'Brien, and the Hon. Arthur Dillon. Two further regiments sent by James – Butler's and Feilding's – were broken up and their men drafted into the other three.

These regiments, and those raised thereafter for the French service, took the name of their titular colonel, or *Mestre-de-Camp Propriétaire*, who effectively 'owned' the regiment. This officer might in practice hold a far higher rank and did not necessarily serve with his regiment. If he were not present in person, command would be invested in a *colonel-commandant*. In order of seniority, the initial three regiments comprised:

- Régiment de Mountcashel, taken into French service in 1690 but tracing its ancestry to an Irish regiment embodied by Charles II in 1683 from Irish garrison troops previously stationed in Tangier. Became in 1694 the Régiment de Lee, and in 1734 the Régiment de Bulkeley by which title it was still known in 1745 the colonel being *Lieutenant Général* François de Bulkeley.

- Régiment O'Brien, taken into French service in 1690 but raised the previous year for James II. Became Régiment de Clare in 1691 upon its colonel becoming 4th Viscount Clare, and then the Régiment de Lee in 1693 after Clare's death. Andrew Lee transferring the following year to the former Régiment de Mountcashel, it became the Régiment de Talbot, and on Talbot being disgraced in 1696 and stripped of his commands it passed to the brother of its original colonel and, he now being 5th Viscount, became again the Régiment de Clare. From 1706 to 1720 again the Régiment O'Brien, the colonelcy passing to a junior branch of the family, until the 6th Viscount Clare came of age and assumed the colonelcy in the latter year and the Clare name was once again restored. A *lieutenant général* by 1745, and, as noted, the man responsible for introducing Charles to the coterie of Franco-Irish ship-owners who got the prince to Scotland, Clare is often referred to in French sources as the Comte de Thomond in reflection of the family's claim to the Irish earldom of that name of which they had been deprived in 1691.

- Régiment de Dillon, taken into French service in 1690 having recently been raised for James II. Unlike the two previous, this unit never changed its title. The initial colonel – who eventually died in 1733 as a *lieutenant général*, having been created Comte de Dillon in the French nobility and Earl of Dillon in the Jacobite peerage – was succeeded by his sons one after another: Charles de Dillon, and his brother Henri after him following Charles' early death, resigned the colonelcy so as to pursue their claims to family lands in Ireland; the third brother, the Chevalier Jacques de Dillon succeeded in his turn but was killed at the head of the regiment at Fontenoy so that by the time of the '45 it was the fourth brother, Edouard de Dillon, who held the role.

In the long run, of course, French help availed James II nothing and his Irish realm was lost along with the rest. From the troops who followed him into exile after the 1691 Treaty of Limerick – the so-called 'Wild Geese', although the term quickly became attached to the Jacobite Irish diaspora as a whole – James built up an army-in-exile which fought alongside French troops in the remaining battles of the War of the League of Augsburg before finally being disbanded as part of the peace settlement that ended that conflict. From its veterans, more regiments were formed for the regular French service to join Mountcashel's original three. The Régiment de Galmoy was disbanded at the end of the War of the Spanish Succession, and the Régiment de Bourke transferred to the Spanish service, but two other infantry units survived which lasted through to serve in the 1740s along with one regiment of cavalry:

- Régiment de Dorrington. Taken into the French service in February 1698, but tracing its ancestry back, through James II's Royal Irish Regiment of Foot Guards, to the Royal Irish Regiment formed by Charles II in 1662. From 1718 Régiment de Rooth, the colonel in 1745 being *Maréchal de Camp* Charles Edouard Lesley, Comte de Rooth, who had succeeded his father to the position in 1733.
- Régiment de Berwick. Raised 1698 for the French service out of the disbanded Regiment of Foot of Athlone, King's Regiment of Dismounted Dragoons, and Independent Companies of Foot, all from James II's exile army. Its first colonel was James Fitzjames, Duke of Berwick, illegitimate son of James II by Arabella Churchill (and therefore nephew of the 1st Duke of Marlborough), and the regiment remained in his family after the Duke's death, retaining the Berwick title although the 2nd Duke – the only child of Berwick's first marriage – had relocated to Spain. Its colonel in 1745 was *Maréchal de Camp* Edouard, Comte de Fitzjames, fifth son of the 1st Duke's second marriage. Reflecting the close-knit ties that bound the Jacobite exile community, his mother was born Anne Bulkeley, sister to the colonel of the regiment of that name.
- Régiment de Sheldon. Raised 1698 for the French service out of the cavalry of James II's army-in-exile. From 1706 Régiment de Nugent, and from 1733 Régiment de Fitzjames. The title of Duc de Fitzjames was created in 1710 by Louis XV for the 1st Duke of Berwick and the succession passed to his sons by his second marriage; the colonel with whom we are concerned here was *Maréchal de Camp* Charles de Fitzjames, the fourth son of that marriage, who would in due course succeed to the ducal title after the death of his three elder brothers.

The above six regiments constituted the Irish contingent of the French army throughout the War of the Polish Succession and remained in existence after that conflict ended; however, with Europe again descending into war in the 1740s, two more regiments were raised.

- Régiment de Lally. Raised 1744 out of surplus manpower left over from the reduction of the established strength of the five Irish infantry regiments then in existence. Thomas, Comte de Lally, the new regiment's colonel, had previously been an officer of the Régiment de Dillon.
- Régiment Royal Ecossois. Authorised in 1743 and embodied the following year under the colonelcy of Lord John Drummond, younger brother of James Drummond, titular 3rd Duke of Perth. Like Lally, Lord John had previously been an officer of the Régiment de Dillon.

This, then, completed the roster of the Irish Brigade in 1745. In terms of their internal make up, all seven infantry regiments were organised with a single battalion only; this was in contrast to the bulk of French infantry line regiments which were organised on a multi-battalion basis with some having as many as four battalions in the field. Not since Louis XIV's time had the Irish regiments fielded multiple battalions, however. The battalion structure in force, as of 1744 when the establishment was modified, consisted of a staff, 12 companies of fusiliers, and one company of grenadiers. The staff of a single-battalion regiment comprised the *colonel, lieutenant-colonel, major, aide-major,* two *enseignes* (ensigns; to carry the regimental colours), *chirugien* (surgeon), and *aumônier* (chaplain). The post of *major* was somewhat different to what might be implied by the equivalent rank in the British service, the role being more akin to that of an adjutant. The *major* was the officer primarily responsible for the day-to-day running of the battalion, with the *aide-major* to assist him. These posts were present in all French battalions, whether national or foreign; however, the Régiment Royal Ecossois in addition maintained an interpreter on the regimental staff.

The fusilier companies – the standard term for line infantry in the French service, from the *fusil* or musket that they carried; the equivalent would be the hatmen of a British battalion – were all organised on a structure of one *capitaine,* one *lieutenant,* eight *bas-officiers* (NCOs), one *tambour* (drummer), and 40 fusiliers. In two of the companies, the position of *capitaine* was nominally filled by the colonel and lieutenant-colonel respectively, the *lieutenant* commanding the company while they exercised their higher functions. The *bas-officiers* comprised two *sergents,* three *caporaux,* and three *anspessades*; the first two ranks should be self-explanatory, whilst the latter equated to the later British ranks of chosen man or lance corporal. The grenadier company was established as above, but had a *sous-lieutenant* as an additional commissioned officer and a slightly higher rank and file establishment of 45 grenadiers.

In addition to the regularly-established companies, a battalion on campaign maintained an extra company known as the picquet. This formation was created by drawing officers and men from the fusilier companies of the battalion, and could be employed for a variety of tasks – maintaining a camp guard, garrisoning a post, reinforcing the grenadiers if required for a dangerous task (the Royal Ecossois did this for the Battle of Falkirk), or providing troops for detached service under which circumstances picquets from several battalions could be combined to form a provisional unit. It was the last option that led to the formation of the Irish Picquets as a composite battalion to go to Scotland. The *Code Militaire* of 1755 formalised the composition of a picquet as being one *capitaine,* one *lieutenant,* two *sergents,* one *tambour,* and 48 rank and file (including *caporaux* and *anspessades*). The record of men taken prisoner from the picquets of Berwick, Bulkeley, and Clare that were captured at sea on the way to Scotland, analysed below, would suggest that the rank and file strength of the 1745 picquets was on a par with this. The picquet of the Régiment de Berwick that landed at Peterhead on 25 February 1746 is recorded as being 46-strong, but it is not clear whether or not this figure includes officers and *sergents.*

The other point to note about the picquets sent to Scotland was that they had just over double the quota of officers outlined in the 1755 specifications. One of the reasons for this was that spare officers were needed for liaison duties with the Jacobites and for secondment to help organise and train the Jacobite levies. However, it is also true that the Irish Brigade had something of a surfeit of officers, with additional *capiatines-en-second* and *lieutenants-en-second* over and above the establishment. These so-called *officiers reformés* – the term echoes the reformadoes found in 17th century British armies – had no formal place in the structure of a battalion but did duties as supernumeraries. In theory they were awaiting a vacancy in the regular establishment, but in practice their maintenance served as a means of providing an employment and pension for members of the Jacobite exile community. The needs of the community were also served by the provision of posts for *cadets* – would-be officers in training, for whom there was the generous allowance of 16 per regiment – and *volontaires* – gentlemen-rankers serving without pay in the hope of obtaining a commission.

French infantry drill called for the battalion to be formed up as a four-deep line, which for all ranks to be able to fire required the first and second ranks to kneel. A battalion could be divided into platoons for alternate firing; however, a tactical preference for volleys by rank or by the whole battalion remained prevalent. There was also a preference for the employment of shock action with cold steel rather than prolonged firing. Officially, troops did not march to the cadence of a drum-beat, the drums being retained for signalling, but it is likely that, as with many apparent innovations of the 1750s, the introduction of the cadenced step at that point was the formalisation of a practice that was already common and that the cadence was in fact employed in the 1740s.

Although James II's army-in-exile retained English as the language of command, this was not the case for those units taken into the regular French service. This is not, however, as illogical as it may seem, for a number of reasons. Firstly, as we shall see, the ethnic and linguistic composition of the Irish Brigade by the 1740s was somewhat mixed, with no obvious common language, and some of the second- and third-generation Franco-Irish officers seem not to have had much English in any case: it is noted, for example, that *Lieutenant* Nicolas Glascoe of the Régiment de Dillon, an officer who would play a significant role in the '45, was a native French-speaker and only began to learn English at all when commissioned into the regiment.[1] Secondly, it would on occasion be necessary for Irish troops to cooperate directly with French national troops, for which the ability to follow French orders and drill commands would be essential. Thirdly, the ability to understand drill orders in a foreign tongue does not in and of itself assume a complete familiarity with that tongue; one simply has to associate the sounds with the required drill movement, and in that sense the sounds of '*haut les armes*' are no more alien to a recruit, of any linguistic background, than 'order your firelocks'. Just because the troops drilled in French, however, should not be taken imply that they spoke it exclusively – or even at all, as the presence of the Royal Ecossois' interpreter confirms.

The organisation of the Régiment de Fitzjames reflected that of the French cavalry as a whole, having a regimental staff and four squadrons. The staff was much like that of an infantry battalion, having the *colonel*, *lieutenant-colonel*, *major*, *aide-major*, *chirugien*, and *aumônier*; there were in addition a kettledrummer and four *hautbois* (musicians). Each squadron was

---

1    Helen C. McCorry, 'Rats, Lice and Scotchmen: Scottish Infantry Regiments in the Service of France', 1742-62, *JSAHR*, Vol.LXXIV No.297 (Spring 1996), p.3.

formed of four companies, and each company had a *capitaine*, a *lieutenant*, a *cornette*, a *maréchal de logis* (senior sergeant, somewhat akin to the troop-quartermasters of contemporary British cavalry regiments under which denomination they appear in some of the prisoner listings), two *brigadiers* (NCOs; the rank being more akin at this time to a junior sergeant than to its later application as a corporal of horse), a *trompette* (trumpeter), and, from 1742, an establishment of 35 *maîtres* (troopers). Two to four *maîtres* per company were designated as *carabiniers*, having elite status akin to the infantry grenadiers. In action, the squadron was drawn up in three ranks. Tactical doctrine emphasised cold steel; whilst not formally prohibited, the use of firearms in pitched battle had fallen out of fashion, these being retained for skirmishing. However, the charge was carried out at a walk or trot rather than at the gallop, relying on the mass effect of tight ranks and the weight of horseflesh to break the enemy.

At the outbreak of the War of the Austrian Succession, the five Irish infantry regiments in existence at that time were brigaded together for the first time in decades, creating an Irish Brigade in a tactical as well as an organisational sense. As such they served in the Dettingen campaign of 1743 where they had the good fortune not to form part of the contingent that crossed the Main to defeat at the hands of the allies. In 1745, the new regiments of Lally and Royal Ecossois having taken to the field, all seven infantry regiments were brigaded together as part of Maurice de Saxe's army in Flanders under the command of Viscount Clare. Here the six Irish regiments took part in the Battle of Fontenoy where they famously charged as part of the counterattack that repelled the massed Anglo-Hanoverian column that Cumberland had driven into the heart of the French defences. The Régiment Royal Ecossois was not present at the battle, being detached as part of the covering force for the siege of Tournai; the Régiment de Fitzjames was brigaded with French troops as part of the cavalry First Line. Although a great deal is made of the Irish Brigade at Fontenoy in English-speaking accounts, much has been exaggerated: *Sergent* Wheelock of the Régiment de Bulkeley did not, for example, capture a colour of the Coldstream Guards, but, it would seem, one belonging to the less prestigious Sempill's 25th Foot. Conversely, the role of French units, notably the Régiment de Normandie and a large portion of the French heavy cavalry, in defeating Cumberland's attack, is often forgotten outside of the Francophone world.

Indeed, in the immediate aftermath of the battle a pamphlet-war developed as Irish officers sought to establish their own position as the architects of victory and their French opposite numbers made their own claims and counter-claims. This is worth mentioning, not only because it casts some doubt on the fondly-held idea that the Irish Brigade were the recognised elite troops of the French army at this time but also because it emphasises the fact that the exiled Irish military dynasties which provided the core of officers for the brigade were dependent on continued royal patronage for their careers and so any means by which reputations could be inflated, and those careers thereby advanced, needed to be taken. A fine example of this is the description of Nicolas Glascoe as 'a good officer who has need of the King's grace to support his family'.[2] It was important for such officers that they, and their regiments, did not lose out on their share of credit and glory – even if this meant bandying words with the celebrated Voltaire, whose account of Fontenoy was felt to have unjustly slighted the Irish contribution.

It would be to go somewhat too far to suggest that the Irish Brigade regiments existed purely as a means of providing a place and pension for Jacobite exiles and their descendants, but this aspect certainly played a role in the continued existence of the regiments, and helps explain both why so many *officiers reformés* were maintained on the strength and why the number of units was not only kept up into the 1730s, and even expanded in the 1740s, at the same time as the number of authentically Irish and Scots recruits for the rank and file was beginning to decrease. So serious, indeed, had this deficiency become that in 1744, when the polite fiction that French troops were in the field as auxiliaries of the Elector of Bavaria was at last dropped and war against Britain formally declared, a Royal Ordonnance was issued *'Pour obliger les Anglois, Ecossois & Irlandois qui sont en France, de prendre parti dans les Régimens Irlandois qui son ten service de Sa Majesté'* (that is to say, 'To oblige the English, Scots, and Irish who are in France, to join the Irish regiments in the service of His Majesty'); in order to ensure that those in question did oblige, the alternative to enlistment was condemnation to service in the galleys.

This discrepancy between the origins of the officers and of the men they led is one that becomes apparent when one studies the available lists of the troops, which reveal a surprising variety of origins for the men in the ranks, and wide range of reasons for being there. Since the sources for this analysis, and the conclusions that can be drawn from them, differ from unit to unit, each element will be addressed in turn.

### Manpower Analysis – Irish Picquets

For the Irish regiments, we have a little more material to go on since – if we assume that the men sent to Scotland were a representative sample of the manpower of their respective regiments – we can draw evidence from studies of the Irish Brigade as a whole as well as specific analysis of men captured during the events of the '45.

A total of eight picquets were formed to go to Scotland: an initial batch of six, one from each regiment, and then two more from the Régiment de Berwick. Of these, the ships carrying three of the initial six – those of Berwick, Bulkeley, and Clare – were intercepted during their passage by the Royal Navy and the men taken into captivity. Of these, a full record was made when the men were confined as prisoners of war at Hull, which forms the basis for a representative sample of the composition of these detachments when they were sent to Scotland.[3] A further listing exists of men who were

---

2    Quoted in McCorry, 'Rats, Lice and Scotchmen', p.17.
3    'A Return of the Prisoners of Buckly's [*sic*] Clare's and Berwick's Regiments confin'd in the Citadell of Hull', TNA, SP36/89, pp.38-40.

taken prisoner at Culloden – the picquets of Dillon, Rooth, and Lally from the initial shipment, and the second picquet of Berwick (the third was captured after the loss of the privateer *Prince Charles*, along with the gold shipment it was escorting) – but this is incomplete and both reduced by casualties and increased by recruitment of Government prisoners of war whilst the battalion was in Scotland.[4] For both of these reasons it is an interesting document which will be returned to, but it is the Hull list that provides a more representative sample and forms the basis for an initial analysis of the officers and men.

There were 14 officers, 2 officer cadets, and 155 men captured in the three picquets, these being composed as set out in Table 3. However, of these only 127 were investigated by Captain Eyre at Hull and it is not clear what had become of the remainder. Certainly some men who were identified as deserters from the British service had been separated out by this point, since the three who are known to have been executed for this crime – Francis Forbes, John Irvine, and David Welsh – do not appear on Eyre's list; whether this represents all of the missing 28 rank and file personnel is, however, unclear.[5]

Table 3: Composition of the Picquets of Bulkeley, Clare, and Berwick

|  | Bulkeley | Clare | Berwick |
| --- | --- | --- | --- |
| *Capitaine* | 2 | 2 | 2 |
| *Lieutenant* | 4 | 2 | 2 |
| *Cadet* | 2 | 0 | 0 |
| *Sergent* | 2 | 2 | 3 |
| *Caporal* | 3 | 3 | 3 |
| *Tambour* | 1 | 1 | 1 |
| *Fusilier* | 46 | 46 | 47 |

There are in addition listed two surgeons and four servants, regiments unspecified.

Looking first at the officers, it is clear that the picquets were double-officered at the least. Three of the eight *lieutenants* are given by Eyre as '2 Lieut.', presumably being *officiers reformés* and all coming, according to the listing in John Cornelius O'Calaghan's *History of the Irish Brigades in the Service of France*, from the Régiment de Bulkeley. All 18 men were listed in the record of prisoners as having been born in Ireland, but it was noted that *Capitaine* James Conway, although listed as a native of County Kerry, 'Pretends to be a Frenchman', an annotation that is repeated for several of the rank and file prisoners as well. Conway is, however, given in a later list

4    Alistair Livingstone of Bachuil, Christian W.H. Allen, and Betty Stuart Hart (eds.) *Muster Roll of Prince Charles Edward Stuart's Army 1745-46* (Aberdeen: Aberdeen University Press, 1984), pp.134-138.
5    The figure of 158 is a total of the breakdown of non-commissioned prisoners as listed in John Cornelius O'Calaghan, *History of the Irish Brigades in the Service of France* (Glasgow: Cameron and Ferguson, 1885), p.397. Names of executed deserters from Reid, *1745*, pp.103-104.

of officer prisoners as being born at 'Besseau near Lisle, Flanders', so it does seem that he was what he claimed to be.[6] Five of the *capitaines* were in their thirties, but James McGrath was 50 and had been an officer since 1711. Of the five younger men, Conway gave no date for his first service, although the second listing indicates that he had been a *capitaine* since 1740, and Nicholas Morris seems to have given his year of birth rather than his year of first commissioning which is not especially helpful; the others had served for an average of 18 years although in the case of Richard Nagle, aged only 32 but serving since 1725, it is doubtful whether the earliest years of that service were carried out in anything other than the most notional sense as a pre-teen officer would have been of little use even to a peacetime army.

Interestingly, the average age of the eight *lieutenants* was 30, with the eldest, Patrick Magher, at 39 being older than all but one of the *capitaines*; length of service ran from nine or 10 years for several of the junior *lieutenants* including all three of the *lieutenants-en-second*, through to Magher's 23 years; the average service was 13 and a half years. The two cadets, George and Francis Mathew, both from County Tipperary, were 22 and 20 years old respectively and had both served since 1737. This gives an age and service profile almost identical to the block of younger *lieutenants*, suggesting an influx of new officers into the Brigade in the immediate aftermath of the War of the Polish Succession. Conversely, the four oldest *lieutenants*, and all of the *capitaines* for whom we have data, were veterans of that conflict and all the officers and cadets had been with their regiments since before the outbreak of the War of the Austrian Succession.

The two surgeons had also been in service since before the outbreak of the war, although only just in the case of 23-year-old Thomas Hogan from Bealkelly in County Clare who had joined in 1739 when the war clouds were certainly gathering, and whose surgeon's warrant, according to the separate listing of officer prisoners, dated only to 1743. Interestingly, Hogan was known to the British officer tasked with producing an account of the circumstances of the prisoners, Captain Straford Eyre of Battereau's 62nd Foot, Hogan's father having been a servant to the Eyre family. Eyre came from the Protestant Ascendency in Galway, where his father had been Governor of the town (to which post he would himself succeed in 1747), which would suggest that Eyre was chosen for the role of investigating the prisoners because he had an Irish background that would give him some chance of uncovering the circumstances of men suspected of trying to disguise their ancestry or otherwise mislead the investigation. The other surgeon, John Dwyer, was 33 years of age and had served since 1732.

Other than Captain Eyre expressing doubts over Conway's country of birth and commenting that the Hogan family was known to him, the return of prisoners contains no other remarks pertaining to the officers. However, for those of the 127 rank and file identified as hailing from the British Isles – including several identified as such by Captain Eyre's investigations even though the man himself swore blind that it was otherwise – a more detailed

---

6  'Hull a list of the Officers, Prisoner of War with the Place of their Birth and date of Their Commissions', TNA, SP36/89, p.118.

account was taken down of where and by whom each man was enlisted for French service, and their 'Inducement for Going to France'. The purpose of this investigation in 1746 was evidently so that something could be done to shut down any further flow of manpower into the ranks of the Irish Brigade, but for the historian it is of great use in unravelling the origins and motives of the men serving in the ranks.

Of the 127 men – six *sergents*, eight *caporaux*, a solitary *tambour*, and 112 fusiliers – present at Hull, only 101 were subject to Eyre's detailed investigation, the remaining 26 being foreign born. The first important point to note, therefore, is that 20 percent of the sample came from outside the British Isles, which, after making allowance for two Englishmen and six Scots, leaves only 73 percent of the sample as Irish born (four of whom claimed not to be). Of Eyre's pretended Frenchmen amongst the fusiliers, no further information is given but for *Caporal* Brien Fitzgerald Eyre's verdict was specifically noted that 'This is certainly a transport'd Felon or Fled from Justice as he denies his Country', and the captain had a similar but not entirely legible annotation made next to the entry for *Sergent* Gerald Fitzgerald.

The six sergents were all listed as being of Irish birth and aged between 27 and 45, within which, however, three fell into the 27-32 age bracket and the remainder 43-45. The majority had 16 or more years of service, with the exception being Nicholas Dunn, aged only 27, who had nevertheless still served for nine years. Five of the six men were listed as 'Went Purposely to France to Serve', and the sixth, Fitzgerald, claimed to have been born there. These, then, were men who had chosen to make a career in the Irish Brigade and by 1745 were all veteran soldiers who would have served through the opening years of the War of the Austrian Succession.

The eight *caporaux* show a similar profile, again all listed Irish-born and aged between 26 and 40 with an average age of 33. Service averaged 11 years, with some having started at quite a young age: Peirce Coghlan, aged only 26, nevertheless had 11 years of service to his credit which means that he was only 15 when he enlisted at La Rochelle having travelled to France for that purpose. Several of his fellow-*caporaux* had similarly made a conscious decision to make a career in the French service and were willing to admit to doing so. However, two – Felix McCabe from Cavan and Michael McMahon from County Clare – had initially travelled to France to visit relations and had only subsequently elected to enlist; quite possibly these relations were already serving in the Brigade, which may have encouraged the decision, or possibly they represented a convenient cover story to present to Captain Eyre and his investigators. Two of the eight, however, were enlisted in Ireland as part of the covert recruiting process that took place in that country. This seems to have been confined to individual officers and NCOs rather than full-scale recruiting parties – we should not imagine soldiers of the Brigade beating up for recruits in Irish towns and villages – and it is possible that an element of subterfuge was on occasion involved.

Of the two *caporaux* enlisted in Ireland, Edmond Divey from Waterford was a willing-enough recruit, signed up at Kilkenny in 1736 by an unnamed *capitaine* of the Régiment de Bulkeley, but the case of John Malowny of Limerick is rather more complex. For a start, according to Eyre's record, he was enlisted not by an officer of the Irish Brigade but by an 'Officer of Lowendahl's, Terence O'Bryan': this is problematic since the Regiment de Lowendal, a German regiment in French service raised by and for Maurice de Saxe's Danish-born lieutenant, Ulrich Frédéric Woldemar, Comte de Lowendal, was not embodied until 1743 and Malowny was enlisted in 1735. At that time, Lowendal was in the service of the Elector of Saxony and was in fact commanding troops against France in the War of the Polish Succession, so it is possible that O'Bryan was recruiting not for the French service but for the Saxon – if this was concealed, this may explain why Malowny is recorded as having enlisted 'At Cork in Ireland, being decoy'd' – although this fails to explain how it was that Malowny did eventually end up in the Irish Brigade. Alternatively, if Malowny was mistaken over the forename and regiment of the man who enlisted him it could be that the officer concerned was the same individual listed in a later entry as the 'Officer of Bulkeley's Wm. O'Brien' who enlisted Philip Haynes, a native of Tipperary, at Waterford in 1735 by means of getting him drunk and having him carried aboard ship while still under the influence: possibly Malowny was 'decoy'd' in a similar fashion. The name O'Brien continues to occur in the context of dubious recruiting practices; in 1724 *Lieutenant* Daniel O'Brien of the Régiment de Clare enlisted Barry O'Brien by similar means.

Only one of the three *tambours* captured was still with the prisoners when Eyre inspected them, Humphrey Lynch of the Régiment de Bulkeley from Coolmagort in County Kerry who went purposely to Flanders to enlist in 1741 at the age of 16. Other than his relative youth he had much in common with the 78 Irish-born fusiliers: their average age was just under 30, with the majority falling into the 20-40 age bracket, and the average length of service was 10 years; the veteran amongst them was 50-year-old James Maginnis from Dunboyne in County Meath who had enlisted in 1713 and so served for 33 years. In terms of places of enlistment, the total breaks down as per Table 4.

**Table 4: Enlistment Origins of Irish-Born Fusiliers, Picquets of Bulkeley, Clare, and Berwick**

| Enlisted | Total | Percentage |
|---|---|---|
| Ireland | 15 | 19.2 |
| England | 1 | 1.3 |
| Continent, having gone for that purpose | 35 | 44.9 |
| Continent, having gone for other reasons | 21 | 26.9 |
| Claimed to be of French birth | 2 | 2.6 |
| Deserted to the Brigade | 4 | 5.1 |

Of those recruited in Ireland, almost all were signed up by an officer or *sergent* of their future regiment. In one case at least, trickery seems to have been involved, it being recorded of Patrick Plunkett of County Kerry, who was only 16 years old in 1738 when 'Lt. Weyle of Clare's Regt. Listed him in Kerry, seemingly for the King's Army, & took him to France'. However, the majority admitted to being genuine volunteers although some were recruited after drink had been taken, under circumstances suggesting varying degrees of coercion from persuasion whilst under the influence to being Shanghaied and finding oneself on a ship to France as with Fusiliers Haynes and Brien noted above. Coercion also seems to have been involved in the case of Andrew Quishin from Gregamanah in Kilkenny, enlisted in 1738. The full text of the note next to his name is obscured, but the legible passage reads, 'Soldier of Fitz James listed him at Waterford and forced him...' Exactly what he was forced to do is, however, unclear but the fact that the enlister was a common soldier is interesting and unique amongst the examples of enlistment in Ireland. It does, however, reoccur in the case of James Row from Ballina in Tipperary of whom it was noted that a 'Soldier of Bulkeley's named Jno. Carrol listed him in Kent, where he work'd'; similarly, one of the two Englishmen in the sample, 54-year old Robert Power from Andover in Hampshire, was enlisted in 1735 'by a French soldier in London'.

During peacetime, at least, the recruitment of the odd Irishman here and there was tacitly approved of, or at least not interfered with by the authorities. However, a more flagrant attempt could bring down a response. Ross Farrell from County Longford was only 13 when he was enlisted at Dublin in 1731, along with 20 more recruits by a *Capitaine* Moody, who was arrested, tried, and hanged for so doing. Another of Moody's recruits, *Sergent* Christopher Pickering from Athlone, regiment unspecified, ended up as one of 14 Irish and Scots soldiers in French service confined as prisoners at Berwick-upon-Tweed after the '45 who were also investigated by the diligent Captain Eyre where the circumstances of his enlistment, and Moody's hanging, were again recorded.[7]

About those who made their own way to France purposely to enlist, little more remains to be said. As with their non-commissioned counterparts, these were clearly genuine volunteers who sought to make a career in the Irish Brigade. Those who went – or claimed they went – to the Continent for other reasons and were only then persuaded to enlist are a rather more varied group. Some, certainly, seem to have professed innocent motives for traveling to France even though their circumstances suggest otherwise; John Hacket from Kilmanagh, for example, claimed that he 'Went to see relations' but enlisted into the Régiment de Bulkeley at Nantes, apparently straight off the boat. Other accounts have more of a ring of truth to them. Patrick Fitzpatrick from Dublin was sent to study at St Omer – presumably at the Jesuit English College there – but was instead recruited there by an officer of the Régiment de Bulkeley. Mark Flannady, from Sixmilebridge in County Clare 'Went to France a servant, & his master dying, he listed' at Valenciennes into the Régiment de Clare; similarly, Thomas Daly from Tralee 'Went from Dublin a Servant to a Mr Richard Brown Esquire' and from that employment became servant to *Capitaine* Conway. William McCarty from Ballykilbeg in County Down and Michael Keighry from Tubberpadder in County Galway were both on board ships that were carried into Nantes by bad weather; enlisting there in 1736 and 1740 respectively. Appearing in the case of Hackett, above, and mentioned as a place of enlistment by a number of the self-confessed

---

7    'A List of the Prisoners Confin'd in Berwick', TNA, SP36/89, p.40.

genuine volunteers, thanks to its location Nantes was a key recruiting station for the Brigade.

The last group of Irish recruits were those who deserted to the French service from other armies. In the case of William McDool from Saint Johnstown in Donegal, doing so actually got him back to where he wanted to be, the annotation recording that he 'Deserted from ye Dutch to get home. Was inlisted [*sic*] for Rothes [ie the Régiment de Rooth] & sold to the Dutch'; having made his escape he enlisted into the Régiment de Clare at Alost in 1744. The selling of recruits to the Dutch – who needed men from the British isles to keep up their Scots Brigade – was clearly not restricted to French recruiters; John Courtney from Ballynery in Armagh thought that he was joining King George's Army when he signed up in 1745, but instead of finding himself in the 21st Royal North British Fusiliers as he had expected he was, like McDool, sold into the Dutch service from which he promptly deserted. Going over to the enemy lines, he was enlisted into the Régiment de Berwick at Alost from where he must almost immediately have been selected to do duty with the Picquet being prepared to go to Scotland. John Magrath, from Athy in County Kildare, was another deserter from the Dutch service, but if his service in the army of the United Provinces was involuntary he made no mention of it.

If we discount Courtney's abortive attempts to enlist in the 21st, only one man in the batch of prisoners had worn King George's red coat before donning King Louis', and that was 27-year-old Thomas Foster from King's County, late of the 23rd Royal Welsh Fusiliers. Foster claimed to have been taken prisoner at Fontenoy, but he also claimed to have served since 1743 or '44, a set of dates that do not match up: possibly he was giving the date of his enlistment into the British service. As noted, however, other known deserters had already been extracted from the prisoners before Eyre inspected them and so the actual proportion of former British soldiers would in fact have been much higher than the presence of this one man suggests; indeed, what is more remarkable is that Foster had managed to conceal his circumstances up until this point.

Deserters from the Dutch service also supplied the six Scotsmen amongst the prisoners, aged between 22 and 36 and all of them listed as 'Deserted from ye Scotch Dutch', whilst the other Englishman amongst the collection was an ex-sailor, 21-year-old James Edworth from Petworth in Sussex, whose ship was captured in 1742 and who was enlisted into the Régiment de Bulkeley in Paris. Although this enlistment predates the formal order to impress all inhabitants of the British Isles present within France, it is likely that an element of coercion may have been involved in the recruitment of men in Edworth's position and, to digress for a moment from the study of the Hull prisoners, a number of ex-sailors are recorded amongst the deserters from the Irish Brigade who surrendered themselves to the British authorities in Flanders in the years prior to the '45.

It should of course be recognised that deserters form a self-selecting sample of a regiment and that their circumstances should not be taken as being typical of the whole. Nevertheless, some interesting stories appear when these men's accounts are studied:

Sailors

Deserters from Lally's Regiment

John Jacob, a black taken in a Virginia ship, listed at St John's in Gascoigne last
February by one Captn. Mackraw of Lally's Regiment.

Isaac Cumberland, a Black taken in a Virginia ship, called the Duke of Argyle,
bound for England, listed last Christmas at Brest by one Captn. Haggerty of
the above Regt.

James Stockdel, born at London taken on board the Bacchus Privateer.

Joseph Tibbet, born in Northamptonshire, taken on board the Dolphin Privateer.

Philip Crowden, born in Devenshire taken on board the Dolphin.

James Cowdrey, born at Malden in Essex were all listed some Weeks after, last
Christmas, at Brest by the said Captn. Haggerty.

Richard Masterson, a Cabin boy taken, on board the Alexander Snow, bound
form Cork to the West Indies, was hired by Captn. Mackraw as a servant, &
afterwards turned into the ranks as a soldier.

Sailors

Deserters from Clare's Regiment

Francis Roe, Born in Cork, taken on board the Caesar Privateer of Cowes, was
listed last February at Dinan, by one Captn. Murtach O'Brien of Clare's Regt.

James Rivers, born at London taken aboard the Farmer Privateer of Bristol was
listed last October at Marles in Britany by the above Captn. O'Brien.

Matthew Burras, a Sailor, who was on board the Mediator Sloop, which he says
was lost in the mouth of the Harbour of Ostend at the beginning of the Siege,
he likewise says he served during the Siege as a Gunner in the Town marched
to Ghent with the Garrison, where he left them, came to the French camp,
where he listed in Clare's Regt. from which he deserted in four Days.[8]

As the last case makes clear, these men were not willing recruits and it is
therefore surprising that any such were included amongst the men being
prepared for service in Scotland. However, it is clear that the initial batch
of picquets did include such men – we have already encountered *Fusiliers*
Foster and Keighry amongst the picquets captured at sea, the one a recently
pressed prisoner of war and the other a stranded seaman – and there were
clearly also no qualms about including British deserters amongst that body
either. In any case, when more troops were proposed to be sent and the
whole regiment earmarked for service, the option for prioritising manpower
no longer existed. The following account, which also gives some idea of the
treatment that such men were subjected to in the hope of encouraging their
enlistment, is that of 22-year-old John Unkles of Kidderminster, Worcester,
late of Cottrell's 6th Marines, given at Deal on 28 March 1746:

On oath declares that he was on board His Majesty's Ship Anglesea when she was
taken into France and Carry'd into Port Louis where they were put into a Dungeon
& from thence carry's to Donant and there Confined in the same manner, where

---

8    'List of Deserters examined by Major Leslie the 8th September 1745', TNA, SP87/19, pp.316-
318.

they had very little, were [sic] several of them dyed from the want of Provisions and nastiness of the place; which Obliged this deponent upon the encouragement promised him, and being made drunk, to Inlist in Col'l Lally's Regim't, were [sic] he has continued for Eight Months past he says he was at Boulogne when the last Embarkation was intended when that was laid aside, was March'd to Abbeville and about 6 Weeks since, came with the Regim't to Boulogne again, in order to be Transported to Scotland, but he an nine more between nine and 10 last night seiz'd a Fishing Boat that lay on the Beach without the Place and row'd away for England and landed at Deale about two this afternoon.[9]

Unkles' testimony, although containing some confusing detail about 'the Pretender' being present in command of the two battalions being prepared at Boulogne – the royal person was rather the younger brother, Prince Henry – does confirm that the regiment was under orders for Scotland. Among his companions, and also swearing a testimony of his service was Jacob Daws of Christchurch, another crewman from the *Bacchus* privateer from which James Stockdel in the list above was also pressed.

If the treatment that was employed to persuade Unkles and his comrades to enlist was harsh, so too was that employed in Scotland to bolster the manpower of the Irish Picquets and replace some of the men captured during the sea passage. There are only 34 rank and file prisoners listed amongst the recorded names of those taken after Culloden; one of them is identified as an artilleryman, leaving us to assume the remainder to be from the picquets of Dillon, Lally, Rooth, and Berwick although the regiments are not always specified. Of these, nine are given as Irish, eight as Scots, five English, one French, and 10 unspecified – of the latter, the bulk of the names suggest that the men were from the Britsih Isles although, equally, it is fair to assume that Phillipe Francois, servant to *Capitaine* Burke, and Pierre Poiteu were not.[10] Of the Scots, four were listed as officers' servants, and for the two of these where an age was given both were in their early teens. These were presumably boys engaged after landing in Scotland and it is debatable whether these men should be counted as true soldiers or not, although this did not save 14-year-old John McDonald from transportation. On the other hand, no such annotation is made for the other four Scots, but nor is it clear whether they were local recruits or men who came over with their picquets; the same goes for 22-year old Edward Morris from London. However, the other four Englishmen were all listed as deserters, two apiece from Guise's 6th Foot and one each from Wolfe's 8th and from 'Scott's' – it is unclear which regiment is signified by the latter, since none had a colonel of that name at this time.

Only one of these deserters, the Devonian Samuel Diamond, serving in the Régiment de Rooth but late of Wolfe's 8th, is identified as belonging to

---

9  Testimony in TNA, SP87/82 Part II, p.98. HMS *Anglesea*, a small two-decker of 44 guns, was captured on 28 March 1745, off Kinsale, so the dates of Unkles' testimony do largely fit the narrative.

10  Livingstone of Bachuil et al. (eds.), *Muster Roll*, pp.134-138; it is not clear if Francois' master was John Burke of the Regiment de Clare, or Richard Burke of the Regiment de Dillon, both of whom were taken prisoner at the same time.

a specific Irish Brigade regiment, suggesting, perhaps, that he had deserted some time previously and come over with the French troops whereas the other three had been acquired during the recent campaign. That two of the three were from Guise's certainly fits with this assumption, since that regiment did not serve on the Continent but was instead employed to garrison the Highland forts, several large detachments being captured when Inverness and Fort Augustus were surrendered. According to figures provided by the Marquis d'Eguilles, these four named individuals were amongst some 148 press-ganged prisoners and deserters serving in the ranks of the Irish Picquets at Culloden, 81 of whom were taken prisoner in the battle's aftermath. In the region of 28 of these were executed, their desertion evidently having been flagrant and unmitigated by extenuating circumstances. The majority of the remainder, however, were released without charge and returned to their regiments after neutral testimony made it clear that they had been treated abominably to force them to enlist. In this, therefore, the two men from Guise's named in the muster roll – John Smith of Derby and John Edward Thomas of Shropshire – were unusual in that both were transported.

What is remarkable, if Eguilles' figures are right, is that the Irish Picquets fought as well as they did at Culloden with so many new and unwilling recruits in the ranks. For the bulk of the campaign, however, the battalion was unencumbered with these extra men, who were acquired in significant numbers only during its closing stages. Returning, therefore, to the list of prisoners at Hull to complete our sample of the men sent to Scotland rather than recruited after arrival, the last group of men to consider are those from outside the British Isles, 26 in total of whom three were Dutch and the remainder French. For these men, fewer details are recorded, only name, age, and the fact that all were private soldiers. Interestingly, a number of the names of these men are indisputably non-French in origin – Charles Walsh, Jacob Pinker, James Robeson – and others very possibly French adaptations of Irish or English names. How Captain Eyre came to accept these men as French whilst denying the claims of other prisoners in the list is not clear. The average age of these men comes to 26, a little lower than the average for the Irish-born recruits. Charles Walsh was the veteran amongst them at the age of 50; conversely, Joshua Dubois was only 13. If the French-born men with non-French names are assumed, as would seem likely, to have been men 'Bred up in the Regiment' – to borrow the phrase used to describe *Caporal* Andrew Connell from the Berwick-upon-Tweed consignment of prisoners – then the remainder, leaving aside the Dutch who were presumably deserters from their own country's army, must be assumed to be recent recruits taken into service to make up for the lack of genuine Irish recruits. That this had become necessary was a known concern even before the '45, in that the officers of the Walloon regiments in French service had made an official complaint that the Irish regiments were encroaching on their manpower. An order was initially given to send such men to the Walloon regiments and henceforth recruit only natives of the British Isles, but this was rescinded after protests from the Irish officers; many of the men listed as French, and not possessed of Irish names, may therefore be assumed to most likely represent inhabitants of French Flanders.

This last point, therefore, helps us grasp the character of the Irish Brigade at this turning point in its history. A core still remained of genuine Irish volunteers who actively sought to follow a military career in the French service. These men provided the Irish regiments with their officers and NCOs, as well as the core of their rank and file, but represented a finite resource. The outbreak of the War of the Austrian Succession had effectively cut off the flow of further recruits, and thus there was no way to replace casualties and wastage from the traditional sources. Thus, already by 1745 it had become necessary to enlist a sizeable proportion of non-Irish manpower; not just stray Englishmen and Scotsmen, many of them unwilling recruits brought in under compulsion, but miscellaneous Frenchmen as well. With the investigations carried out by Captain Eyre into the means by which Irish recruits found their way to France marking the beginning of a British Government crackdown on recruiting in Ireland for foreign service, the glory days of the Irish Brigade were over and its regiments would see a marked decline in their fame and fortunes after the end of the war.

## Manpower Analysis – Régiment de Fitzjames

The sources for analysing the Irish cavalrymen in the '45 are very similar to those available for their infantry counterparts: a short listing in the published *Roll Call*, consisting largely of officers and 'quartermasters' – presumably *marechaux de logis* – but also including eight rank and file, and the fruits of another investigation carried out by the indomitable Captain Eyre. This one took place at Canterbury and listed a total of 58 rank and file prisoners along with a 59th who had made his escape before Eyre had a chance to interrogate him.[11] A useful contrast, however, can be made between the data from these sources and those for the whole regiment as it stood shortly before the outbreak of war, based on an exhaustive study of the 1737 *contrôle des troupes* carried out by Eoghan Ó Hannracháin and published in *The Irish Sword*.

Based on the names and known details of those taken prisoner at or after Culloden, and the details provided in Ó Hannracháin's study, there is little doubt but that the regiment was largely officered by men of the same sort of Irish and Franco-Irish background as identified for the Irish infantry. Only in Ó Hannracháin's listing of the regiment's Fontenoy casualties do the names of *Capitaine* Jacqueville and *Aide-Major* Couraix, the former killed and the latter wounded, stand out from amongst the list of Byrnes, Bettaghs, Nugents, and Taaffes. A number of the officers listed in 1737 were, however, of considerable – if not extreme – age, underlying the fact that many of these men had nowhere else to go. *Cornette* Arthur Garvey, for example, was admitted to the *Hôtel des Invalides* in 1744 at the age of 78 and had served since 1702;[12] hardly the impression of the downy-cheeked subaltern that his rank conjures up. This

---

11  'A Return of the Prisoners of Fitzjames's Regiment of Horse, now Confin'd at Canterbury', TNA, SP36/89, pp.5-6.
12  Eoghan Ó Hannracháin, 'An analysis of the Fitzjames Cavalry Regiment, 1737', *The Irish Sword*, Vol.XIX (1993-95), p.257

seems to have been part of a thinning-out of older officers unfit for wartime service, but it was not a given that their replacements were an improvement other than in terms of age. *Capitaine* Robert Shee obtained his promotion to that grade in 1743 and served at Culloden, but it was later reported of him that he was extremely avaricious – a problem when cavalry companies were run on a proprietary basis, placing considerable responsibility in the hands of their captains – and that this had led to complaints against him by his troopers.[13] Still, those complaints were made in the years after the '45, when it must have been clear that Shee's financial prospects outside the regiment were limited indeed.

Of the 58 men investigated by Eyre at Canterbury, who came from that portion of the regiment captured during the sea passage rather than from that which fought at Culloden, 11 were listed as corporals – presumably in fact being *brigadiers* – and the remainder as troopers. The manner in which the circumstances of these men were recorded differed slightly from that employed when Eyre was investigating the infantry, personal details being taken down in the same way but with the additional listing of the man's pre-enlistment occupation, along with a column detailing 'By Whom Listed, & where they embark'd for France'. This means that we do not have the useful distinction that exists in the listing of infantry prisoners between those who made their way to France purposely to enlist and those who travelled there for other reasons and only then persuaded to sign up – or, at least, who claimed that this had been the case.

Of the 11 *brigadiers*, all were Irish-born with an average age of 40 and an average of 18 years of prior service. The bulk of the men fall fairly close to this mean, with the obvious outliers being Morgan O'Brien from Limerick Town, who was 53 years old and had enlisted as far back as 1708, and Robert Lacy from Newcastle in Limerick who was only 23 and had served for only five years. Two other men were also in their twenties, but had rather longer service having enlisted in their mid-teens. One man gave his prior occupation as merchant and another as clothier, but the remainder listed no previous occupation prior to joining the regiment. With one exception – Thomas O'Brien from Tullagh who had made the passage via Dover in 1735 – all had made their way to France from Irish ports. We therefore have a similar situation here to that seen with the Irish infantry, with a core of Irish career professionals forming the backbone of the regiment's non-commissioned leadership.

The 47 troopers make for an interesting study, averaging of 29 years of age and seven years of service. These averages are, however, a little misleading as a closer study of the listing indicates two main groups. On the one hand, there was a core of veterans mostly in their thirties and forties who had served for 10 years or more. The oldest of these, at 56, was Felix Short from Clogher in County Tyrone but he was a relatively late recruit having enlisted only in 1736 after working as a labourer. Discounting Henry McCarty, born into the regiment and therefore claiming all of his 40 years as time served, the longest adult service came from Richard Tracy, who had enlisted aged 20 and served as many years again; he claimed French birth but it was noted that 'this man

---

13 Ó Hannracháin, 'Fitzjames Cavalry Regiment', p.256

confesses to imbark at Lymerick & probably is a transported Felon'. The longest-serving trooper indisputably not of French birth was John M'Mahon from Ennis, County Clare, with 19 years. Allowing for Tracy's confession, 41 men, or 87 percent, were Irish by birth; of the remainder, McCarty as noted was French born but of Irish extraction, three were Scots, one was English, and the last was from Middlesex County in the Commonwealth of Massachusetts. This prevalence of Irishmen is in line with the figures from 1737, when men of Irish birth made up 84 percent of the total, along with a further eight percent Franco-Irish; however, the predominance of men from the province of Leinster noted by Ó Hannracháin is by no means as pronounced in the 1746 listing.[14]

Of the 41 Irishmen, 28 seem to have been genuine volunteers who had made the passage to the Continent with a view to enlisting. Interestingly, several had done so since the outbreak of war, something not seen in the prisoners from the infantry. Timothy McCarthy from Cork 'Went in a Dutch Merchantman from Dublin to France' in 1743; Luke Walsh from Kilkenny 'imbark'd at Dublin w'th one M'Carty, an Irish French Officer' in 1742; William Lacy from Limerick Town was 'Taken from Lymerick by one Lacose, a French Merchant' as recently as 1745. Perhaps even more flagrant, as late as 1740 *Brigadier* Edmund Kelly, himself amongst the prisoners, was in London actively enlisting men for the regiment, returning to the Continent via Dover with a party of recruits that included James Mourn from West Meath and John Lawless from Leitrim, both of whom ended up in Canterbury gaol along with their recruiter.

On the other hand, a greater number of the Irishmen in the ranks appear to have been there less willingly than seems to have been the case in the infantry, albeit that the Régiment de Fitzjames had not needed to follow the infantry in taking in non-Irishmen in any numbers. It is of course entirely possible that were we to look at the Irish infantry regiments as a whole a similar pattern would emerge that is not indicated in the manpower specifically selected for service in Scotland for which task one would assume that only the most reliable men would be chosen. For the Régiment de Fitzjames, however, since the whole unit was sent, no such screening of manpower would have been possible. Matthew Mehagan, a barber from Limerick Town, was 'Taken at sea, listed in prison', as was Patrick Hughes, a Mason from County Carlow who had been on his way to New England. A further seven men had similar stories, as did one of the three Scotsmen amongst the prisoners, 20-year-old Edmund Bond from Stirling. Seventeen-year-old Irish sailor William Ross from Downpatrick had initially been recruited into the Régiment de Rooth, from which he had deserted; it is not made clear whether he was then forcibly brought back and transferred to another regiment or whether he was simply picked up again by a recruiting party before he could find a way home. He 'petitioned to be listed into Pawlet's Marines', a peculiarly specific request but one repeated by other prisoners including the Scotsman Ross. Hugh Byrne from Leitrim had successfully made his sea passage from Philadelphia, but was enlisted by the Gensd'armes at St Malo when he landed there in 1742.

---

14  Ó Hannracháin, 'Fitzjames Cavalry Regiment', p.259

Plate One

B

B1

A.

D.

C.

Naval and Miscellaneous

A – Compagnie de Maurepas, B and B1 – Sailors, C – Officer of Engineers, D – Artilleryman. Please see Notes on the Plates for further details. (Illustration by Mark Allen © Helion & Co)

Plate Two
Irish Troops
part One

C

A

B

D

D1

A – *Caporal*, Régiment de Dillon, B – *Fusilier*, Régiment de Lally, Marching Order, C – *Fusilier*, Régiment de Rooth, Fatigue Dress, D – *Sérgent*, Régiment de Berwick. Please see Notes on the Plates for further details. (Illustration by Mark Allen © Helion & Co)

Plate Three

A

B

C

C1

D

Irish Troops Two

A – *Capitaine*, Régiment de Rooth, B – *Tambour*, Régiment de Dillon, C – *Maître*, Regiment de Fitzjames, on Mounted Duty,
D – *Maître*, Regiment de Fitzjames, Dismounted. Please see Notes on the Plates for further details. (Illustration by Mark Allen
© Helion & Co)

Advance of the composite French battalion at Falkirk, 17 January 1746, original artwork by Steve Noon. The French battalion, composed of the Picquets of Dillon, Lally, and Rooth, plus a picquet and the grenadier company of the Royal Ecossois, was committed towards the end of the battle to help defeat a dangerous Government counter-attack. Shown here is the centre of the French line, with men of the Picquet of Dillon on the left of the scene and of the Royal Ecossois picquet on the right. The steady advance of the French battalion helped restore the situation, and the French troops spearheaded the final Jacobite attack into the streets of Falkirk itself. (Image © Helion & Co)

Plate Four

B

A

C

D

Royal Ecossois

A – Officer with Colour, B – Officer of Grenadiers, C – Lord John Drummond in Modified Uniform, D – Grenadier. Please see Notes on the Plates for further details. (Illustration by Mark Allen © Helion & Co)

Grenadier officer's cap, associated with the Royal Ecossois. See Chapter 3 for discussion of this item and its provenance. (National Museums Scotland)

French gun crew in action c.1745. (New York Public Library Digital Collections)

Monument to the Irish in French service at Culloden. (Photo by Raymond Finlayson)

Reflecting the fact that France was not the only Continental power where it was possible to for an Irish Catholic to make a military career, 27-year-old Michael M'Guire from Galway had served in the Austrian army until 1743 when he was taken prisoner, and was then enlisted into the French service. The other two Scotsmen amongst the prisoners also came into the regiment via a foreign army, in this case the Dutch which would suggest that they were members of the Scots Brigade. Both men, John Crookshank from Aberdeen and Thomas Manners from Midlothian, had deserted from that service in 1745. Manners insisted that he did so 'intending to return home', and that he enlisted with the French 'with no other view'. Crookshank, perhaps believing that a more concrete gesture was required to re-establish his patriotic bona fides, petitioned 'to be rec'd into the Sea Service'.

It has already been noted that one of the prisoners hailed from the American colonies, this being 26-year-old Job Speen who gave his occupation as farmer but was listed as 'taken at Sea listed in Prison by M Drummond at Port Louis', having sailed from Boston destination unspecified. A transatlantic origin may also be suspected in the case of the one Englishman listed amongst the prisoners, who gave his name as Squire Sammy. Whilst it is impossible to prove, this has the ring of a slave name and it is quite possible – bearing in mind the presence of African American recruits in the Régiment de Lally – that he was also of this ancestry. He was 'Taken in ye Thurloe Privateer of Liverpool', but to set against this he also gave his place of birth as Hadamford [sic – unknown location] in Hertfordshire and his occupation as 'Smith and Farrier'. His occupation would certainly have made him an asset to a cavalry regiment, but traditionally, as indicated in Ó Hannracháin's analysis of the 1737 *contrôle des troupes*, the regiment had maintained black trumpeters as was the fashion in many cavalry regiments of the era. No such men have been located as yet amongst the listings of prisoners, but it is entirely possible that some of the six such men serving in 1737 were still in the ranks eight and nine years later.

In general, therefore, the broad trends seen with the Irish infantry are reflected in their cavalry counterparts with a staple of genuine Irish volunteers providing the commissioned and non-commissioned leadership along with the core of the rank and file, but increasingly topped up by less willing recruits from a broader geographical area. Since the Régiment de Fitzjames had seen far less service prior to 1745 than had the Irish infantry, it had therefore been able to avoid needing to make extensive use of Frenchmen to fill its ranks. However, being committed to the campaign of the '45 in full rather than providing detachments the effects of the manpower lost in Scotland were felt far more acutely afterwards, and the post-Culloden rebuilding of the regiment changed its character almost beyond recognition. By 1748 there were 203 Irish in the ranks, or 37 percent, and less than 60 of them were survivors of the pre-war core of the regiment studied by Ó Hannracháin. Thirty-eight percent of the regiment were now French, and the remainder English, Scots, Germans, and other miscellaneous foreigners. As with the infantry, the service of the Irish cavalry in 1745 marked the last hurrah of the old Irish Brigade.[15]

---

15   Ó Hannracháin, 'Fitzjames Cavalry Regiment', p.259

## Manpower Analysis – Régiment Royal Ecossois

Because the efforts of the redoubtable Captain Eyre did not extend to investigating the prisoners of the Royal Ecossois beyond those who ended up in the mixed batch of prisoners at Berwick-upon-Tweed, the sources that we have to work with on this regiment are a little patchier than for the Irish. On the other hand, the listing in the published *Muster Roll* does provide the names and (mostly) the nationalities of some 54 rank-and-file. This therefore provides a sample to work with of a similar size to that offered for the Régiment de Fitzjames by the Canterbury prisoners investigated by Eyre, albeit without the same level of detail. There is also a useful published study in the shape of an article by Helen C. McCorry in the Spring 1996 *Journal of the Society for Army Historical Research*.

As noted above, the Régiment Royal Ecossois was a new formation, and its activation at a time when France was beginning to take a serious interest in matters Jacobite is no coincidence. Although the new regiment drew a portion of its officers from the regiments of the Irish Brigade, so too were commissions granted to a number of gentlemen who were active Jacobites but not necessarily professional soldiers. In a sense, therefore, what was being done here was to bring together a body of politically committed men who could be counted on to support the Stuart cause once the Rising had begun. Such men were not, perhaps, ever minded to make a career in French service for, in their hopes at least, events were moving towards a conclusion that would restore their rightful Prince back at home. It is telling in this light that a number of officers of the regiment left it before it embarked for Scotland and reverted to their true roles as leaders of the local Jacobites. Viscount Strathallan, formerly a *major* in the regiment, fell at Culloden commanding part of the Jacobite cavalry; John Roy Stuart – poet, adventurer, committed Jacobite and erstwhile *capitaine* of grenadiers – raised the Jacobite Edinburgh Regiment after the capture of that city, and led it throughout the rest of the Rising. The raising of the regiment was something that was clearly taken note of by the British authorities, and an attempt was made in September 1745 to piece together a list of the regiment's officers from the testimony of deserters. This has some omissions when compared to the list of officers assembled by McCorry, which is not helped by the evident difficulty that French (and on occasion English) clerks had with Scots and Irish names. John Roy Stuart, for example, though recorded as 'recruiting in Scotland' in the British list – which he was, albeit for his own new regiment, not the French service – has his name spelled Steward, whilst the French listings include *capitaines* Macferson, Duglas, and – a real oddity – Mutinor D'Hostove, the origin of which is unclear.

Notwithstanding the number of Scots willing to serve in the regiment, it was nevertheless necessary to bring in officers of other nationalities as well; going by the intelligence report of September 1745 there were at least three Irishmen and two Englishmen amongst the *lieutenants*, as well as the Irish *Capitaine* Nicholas Magrath (also listed as Mackraw). This latter, although a veteran with a decade's service to his credit when the regiment was formed, was something of a hard bargain – 'very indisciplined and of the very worst behaviour' according to one report – and seems to have ended up in the regiment via service in the Régiment de Lally, which suggests that he had been palmed off onto that unit when it was raised, and that Lally had palmed him off in turn onto the Royal Ecossois. He does, however, seem to have been an effective recruiting officer, judging by how many times his name appears as having enlisted such-and-such a soldier; then again, if he was a disruptive character, recruiting service might have represented the best way to get him away from his fellow officers.

In general, even allowing for those men who had prior service in the Irish regiments, the level of experience of the officers of the Royal Ecossois was not as high as was the case in the Irish Picquets or Régiment de Fitzjames. Few officers had entered French service before 1740, although John Roy Stuart, for one, came with prior experience in the British Army where he had served as a quartermaster in the Scots Greys before resigning when he failed to obtain an appointment to the then newly-raising Black Watch. *Lieutenants* Duncan Colquhoun and Robert Maxwell had also served in the British Army, in Paulett's 9th Marines and Price's 14th Foot respectively.[16] Neither name appears in the lists of officers of these regiments so it is to be inferred that their service was in the ranks; that and the fact that both were listed as having deserted meant that both were in serious danger if they fell into enemy hands: the aftermath of Culloden saw Colquhoun executed and Maxwell banished. Neither of these last two, however, appear in pre-1745 listings of officers and appear to number amongst the personnel acquired whilst the regiment was in Scotland, a development to which we shall return.

There was, however, a core of Scots professional officers who would hold the regiment together during the campaign. The *lieutenant-colonel* was Lord Louis Drummond of Melfort, a relative of the regiment's colonel and son of the 2nd Earl (or Duke, in the Jacobite peerage) of Melfort for which reason he is often referred to in French accounts as the Comte de Melfort. Two of the *capitaines* functioned as *major* during the campaign in Scotland, Lachlan Cuthbert of Castlehill (first name also given as Launcelot, surname also given as Colbert, and listed as Baron de Colbert et de Castellisle in French sources) and John (or Jean) Gordon; David Nairn, given as *major* in pre-1745 French lists and identified as such in the September 1745 British list put together from the testimony of deserters (in which Cuthbert is shown as a *capitaine* and Gordon not at all), does not seem to have served in Scotland. The *aide-major*, Matthew Hale, was apparently an Englishman.

One of the reasons for sending the Royal Ecossois to Scotland was the hope that the regiment would be able to swell its ranks there; indeed, a second battalion was authorised although in reality the need to replace men captured at sea meant that all new recruits were incorporated into the single existing battalion and no second battalion actually materialised. This, however, complicates any analysis of the regiment's composition based on the listings of prisoners taken from it, as it is rarely possible to establish whether

16  Livingstone of Bachuil et al (eds.), *Muster Roll*, pp.61-2; Colquhoun's regiment is listed as 'Paul's', but this does not match any existing unit of the British Army, Paulett's being the closest match.

a Scotsman in the ranks was a recent acquisition or someone who had come over with the regiment. This also applies to the officers: Duncan Colquhoun and Robert Maxwell have already been noted, and to these men should be added George Hay, a shipmaster from Portsoy, William Maxwell (who, like Robert of that ilk, seems to have been of the Maxwells of Barncleuch from Kirkudbright), and Charles Oliphant, an excise man from Aberdeen, all of whom were commissioned as *lieutenants* during the course of the '45. There seems to have been something pre-arranged about this, for when Oliphant was brought to trial it was recorded:

> He was an officer in the Excise at Aberdeen, and afterwards at Inverness till the rebellion broke out. Saw him at Holyrood House with the rebels in October, 1745, with a small sword by his side and a white cockade in his hat, and he was then waiting until Lord John Drummond's regiment should come over, and he was then to have a commission.[17]

Considering that officers of the regiment were actively recruiting in Scotland ahead of the '45, it does not seem unreasonable that potential candidates for commissions were identified at this time.

With the caveat in mind, therefore, that it is not always clear when the Scotsmen amongst the Culloden prisoners were recruited into the regiment, the rank and file of the regiment may be characterised as somewhat mixed. Only three NCOs are listed in the *Muster Roll*, one *sergent* and two *caporaux*, and these consist of an Englishman, and Irishman, and a Scotsman. The Irishman, 20-year-old John Morgan, was a sailor and presumably an unwilling recruit since he deserted during the campaign; that a man of such youth and background was given non-commissioned rank does suggest that the Royal Ecossois could not rely on the same sort of cadre of career veterans that existed within the Irish regiments. As for the ordinary fusiliers and grenadiers, their backgrounds break down as per Table 5.

**Table 5: Countries of Origin, Royal Ecossois Rank and File Prisoners**

| Birthplace | Number | Percentage |
|---|---|---|
| Scotland | 21 | 38.9 |
| Ireland | 7 | 13.0 |
| England | 3 | 5.6 |
| France | 12 | 22.2 |
| Unknown | 11 | 20.4 |

Of those with unknown birthplaces, if an assumption is made based on the given names – one can, after all, hazard a reasonable guess that Jean Bruilez was French and Alexander McDonald Scots – then these follow in rough proportion to the distribution found in the rest of the sample. Whilst Scotsmen therefore make up the largest group within the sample, they are

---

17  James Allardyce (ed.), *Historical Papers Relating to the Jacobite Period, 1699-1750* (Aberdeen: For the New Spalding Club, 1896), Vol.2, p.402

hardly a majority and, as noted, the proportion in the sample can be assumed to be distorted by men recruited during the '45 which would suggest that the regiment as embodied in 1744 was by no means as Ecossois as its name would imply. Indeed, it had even proved necessary for an order to be issued in that year to arrange a more representative distribution of manpower between the regiments, Saxe ordering that the Irish regiments henceforth only accept English and Irish deserters from the allied armies with all Scotsmen to go to the Royal Ecossois: notwithstanding an apparent objection from Viscount Clare, this division was approved by the Comte d'Argenson.[18]

Eight of the 56 prisoners had deserted from the British Army – some of whom, at least, may be assumed to be men who were picked up whilst in Scotland, press-ganged with the same lack of subtlety employed to swell the ranks of the Irish Picquets – and one, Thomas Henderson from Musselburgh, had deserted from the Dutch service. Ages are rarely given in the listings, but those that are provided range from 14-year-old John Heggans, picked up in Glasgow to act as a servant to one of the officers, to 56-year-old James Dyer of Aberdeenshire. Of the remainder, one man is listed as being in his forties, one in his thirties, and 10 in their twenties.

The bland, and often limited, details given by the compilers of the *Muster Roll* mean that it is necessary to look for other sources to try and establish the personal stories of the men in the ranks, and of how they came to be in the regiment. Major Leslie's September 1745 investigation of the circumstances of men who had deserted from the regiment in Flanders provides some insights and further suggests – albeit with the caveat that deserters, as a self-selecting sample, cannot be considered entirely representative – that the expedients required to bolster the ranks of the Irish Brigade were employed to a far greater extent from the outset in the Royal Ecossois.

> William Inglis, born at Edinburgh declares he was an Apprentice to a Merchant at Edinburg[h] and was engaged by Captain Drummond of Strathalan, to go to the West Indies with him as Supercargo on a Merch't Ship, but that the above Captn. Drummond deceived him; brought him to Dunkirk last December and there obliged him to list as a Soldier, and afterwards made him a Serjeant in Lord John Drummond's Regt., from which he deserted as soon as he had an opportunity.
>
> William Bain, born in the Parish of Rae in the County of Caithness, declares he was enlisted last February at Aberdeen by Lieut. Cameron for the Scotch Dutch, but was brought to Dunkirk and made to serve in Lord John Drummond's Regt.
>
> Alexander Robinson, born at Blair in Athol, declares that he was listed last May at Edinburgh by Lt. Jno. Cunningham, to serve in the Scotch Dutch, but was brought by him to Dunkirk and forced to serve in Lord Jno. Drummond's Regt.[19]

---

18 Argenson to Clare, 28 September (NS) 1744, reproduced in Matthew O'Conor, *Military History of the Irish Nation, Comprising a Memoir of the Irish Brigade in the Service of France; with an Appendix of Offial papers Relative to the Brigade, from the Archives in Paris* (Dublin: Hodges and Smith, 1845), pp.394-395.

19 'List of Deserters examined by Major Leslie the 8th September 1745', TNA, SP87/19, p.316.

That French recruiters could be operating in Scotland as late as December 1744, even by clandestine means, was no doubt a worrying piece of intelligence for the authorities in London and Edinburgh.

As we have already seen from the case of *Caporal* Morgan, the Régiment Royal Ecossois was also a beneficiary, like the Irish regiments, of the orders to impress seaman and others from the British Isles who were in France and unable to give an account of themselves. Irish Sailor Patrick McLean was numbered amongst the Culloden Prisoners, and Major Leslie's record of deserters lists another slew of such men under the heading 'Sailors deserters from Ld. Jno. Drummond's Regt.':

> Thomas Hughes, born at Limerick in Ireland was listed last October by one Sullivan, a Cadet in Lord John Drummond's Regt. whom he left with the Regt. when he deserted.
>
> Lawrence Cotter, born at Cork was listed last February at Dinan by one Smith who was formerly a Serjt. in one of the Regts. of Foot Guards and who is now with Lord Jno. Drummond's Regt.
>
> Barry Gwin, born at Cork listed at the same time, by the same Person with Cotter.
>
> Henry Thorn, born at Swanzey in Wales and James Gregory, born in Scotland were likewise listed by Smith at Dinan
>
> Lawrence Colgen, born at Philipstown in Ireland, was taken on his voyage to Philadelphia, carried into Brest in Septem. last, there listed by an officer of Löwendahl's Regt. and afterwards turned over to Lord Jno. Drummond's Regt.
>
> Peter Downey, born at Lismillen in Ireland taken likewise & carried into Brest in August last and listed into Löwendahl's Regt. and afterwards turned over to Lord Jno. Drummond's Regt.
>
> William Barker, born at Manchester was listed last October at Dinan, by Sullivan the Cadet, in Lord Jno. Drummond's Regt.[20]

Smith, the former guardsman, was evidently an active recruiter, also being mentioned as having enlisted Hugh Curry from Ayr who was amongst the prisoners inspected by Captain Eyre at Berwick-upon-Tweed in 1746. Daniel Cameron and John Mackenzy [*sic*] from that batch of prisoners seem also to have been men of the Royal Ecossois, enlisted by *Capitaine* McGrath, but it is not so obvious from which regiment the other two Scotsmen in this batch of prisoners came; all five were, however, youngish men in their twenties and only Curry had served for more than two-and-a-half years which again underlines the apparent lack of long-service professionals in this regiment.

The picture for the Royal Ecossois, therefore, is somewhat different to what comes across for the Irish Brigade, with – outside of the officer corps – a less pronounced national character and less military experience across all ranks. This reflects the fact that the regiment was far less able than its Irish counterparts to benefit from genuine seekers of a military career, both in terms of many of its officers – whose Jacobite politics meant that service

---

20  'List of Deserters examined by Major Leslie the 8th September 1745', TNA, SP87/19, pp.316-317.

in the regiment was a means to an end rather than an end in itself – and its rank and file who seem to have been far more disparate and unwilling than their Irish counterparts. Nevertheless, as we shall see, these differences do not seem to have adversely impacted upon the performance of the regiment in the field and no distinction in terms of quality seems to have been made by contemporaries between the Royal Ecossois and the Irish Picquets.

**3**

# Uniforms and Equipment

### Infantry Units – Generalities

The basic cut of French infantry uniforms in the 1740s was generally simple and conservative in style, with decorative flourishes and additions to the uniforms of line regiments theoretically prohibited by regulation. Other than in the matter of the base-colour of the coats, foreign infantry regiments followed the same regulations as French national regiments; similarly, artillery and engineer units wore the same basic uniform and the general remarks made here should be taken as applying to them also.

The woollen coat – or *justaucorps* – lacked lapels and was fastened by a single line of 9-12 metallic buttons extending down to just below the waist; as of a royal *ordonnance* of 1736, this had replaced the earlier pattern in which the buttons were continued to the hem of the garment. The skirts of the coat could be pinned back, but contemporary illustrations suggest that this was not done so frequently as seems to have been the case a decade later. Were the coat to be pinned back, the turnbacks would reveal the coat lining, which was woollen serge. The same *ordonnance* of 1736 had also reduced the size of the cuffs, which were to be made in such a fashion as to enable them to be unbuttoned and folded down over the hands in cold weather. The cuffs were officially the only place on the *justaucorps* where the regimental facing colour was to be employed (the vexed issue of collars will be returned to in the sections looking at the various regiments), although a further distinction was enabled through the employment of different shapes of pocket flaps with different combinations of buttons.

Under the *justaucorps* was worn a woollen sleeved waistcoat or *veste*. Again, this had nominally been simplified under the 1736 *ordonnance*, which required that it be plain white and without pockets, but, as with the *justaucorps*, embellishments had begun to creep back in and were formally permitted again as of 1747. The *veste* was shorter than the *justaucorps* – extending only to the mid-thighs whereas the latter came down to the knees – and was likewise closed with a single line of metallic buttons. Many contemporary images of French soldiers show the shirt cuffs as visibly protruding from the sleeves of the veste, but the shirt collar was hidden by the *cravatte* or neck-stock. Images from the 1730s – notably the famous Gudenus manuscript of

1735 depicting French troops in Germany and including several of the Irish regiments – show these tied in florid bows, which appears to have been a fashion of the time, but by the 1740s more sober styles seem to have prevailed.

Legwear consisted of woollen breeches, worn with a pair of gaiters made from heavy white linen canvas.

Headwear for both fusiliers and grenadiers was the ubiquitous black 'tricorne' cocked hat, which was edged with metallic lace. Allowing for a few oddities, none of which are of relevance to the units covered in this volume, units that had brass buttons on the *justaucorps* and *veste* had false-gold hat lace, and those that had pewter buttons had false-silver hat lace. A cockade was worn on the left-hand side of the hat, held in place with a black silk ribbon secured to a metallic button. There was no standardised national cockade; both black and white were worn on service, and some regiments even adopted multi-coloured cockades. Bearing in mind the Jacobite antecedents of the bulk of the units under consideration here, it would seem likely that a white cockade would have been preferred by them under any circumstances but this would have become essential for identification purposes for troops serving in Scotland.

Hair was worn queued back and tied with a ribbon, but the fashion for powdering had not yet taken hold. Soldiers were nominally clean-shaven, although in practice this could allow for several days' growth, but moustaches were sometimes worn. Judging by illustrations from the era, the convention that only grenadiers were permitted moustaches does not seem to have become established and in images from the 1730s and 1740s we see both fusiliers with them and grenadiers without.

When off duty or engaged in hard physical work, the cocked hat was replaced by a fatigue cap or *bonnet de police*. Insofar as can be established from the few depictions that exist, these generally had a woollen body in the same colour as the *justaucorps*, with the lower portion turned up in the regimental facing colour to provide an element of stiffening, although at least one depiction shows the reverse of this colour arrangement. Most also appear to have been finished with a decorative tassel.

NCO rank distinctions had not been completely formalised at this time, and although they were consistent within regiments, differences between regiments still existed. The standard that was eventually adopted in 1747, reflecting what had previously been common but by no means universal practice, was woollen lace around the cuff edging for *anspessades*, woollen lace around the cuff button holes for *caporaux*, and metallic lace around

Fusilier of the Régiment de Bulkeley depicted by Charles Lyall. This figure is dated c.1700-1720, and the buttons running the full length of the *justaucorps* and the lack of gaiters are typical of this era. The cartridge box, or *giberne*, is also of an earlier pattern. Nevertheless, the basic outline of the uniform remained unchanged by the 1740s. (Anne S.K. Brown Military Collection)

Officer of the Régiment de Clare depicted by Charles Lyall. Again, this figure slightly predates the events of the 1740s, but the only major difference is that in later years the buttons did not extend the full length of the waistcoat and *justaucorps*. Lyall has also omitted to show the officer's gorget, but gives a good representation of his spontoon. (Anne S.K. Brown Military Collection)

the cuff edging for *sergents*. The woollen lace was white for regiments sporting the pewter buttons/silver lace combination, or yellow for those wearing brass and gold – it is, however, unclear what solution was employed by units such as the Régiment de Berwick who had pewter buttons and white cuffs.

Officers were required to purchase their own uniforms, which followed the colour combinations of their regiments but were of a finer cut and cloth, with real gold or silver for the buttons and hat lace. The *veste*, but not the *justacorps*, was also laced. A gilt gorget was worn when on duty. This was generally plain and undecorated; the embellishment of the gorget with the arms of France did not become common until the middle of the century. Sashes were not worn.

Officers of the Irish Brigade who were seconded to units of the Jacobite army adopted civilian dress including the wearing of tartan sashes. It would seem that this was not entirely popular: *Capitaine* Robert Stack, who commanded the picquet of the Régiment de Lally wrote in January 1746 that he was

pleased to be in command of a picquet which will keep its uniform, otherwise I would have to dress myself in the Highland style, march without breeches, and wear a little bonnet instead of a hat… It is not that I would be ashamed to appear in Highland dress, but I prefer my own.[1]

Furthermore, as we shall see, wearing civilian clothes also placed anyone captured in such attire in considerable jeopardy as dispensing with King Louis' uniform dispensed also with the protection it carried with it.

## Infantry Units – Weapons and Equipment

The standard French infantry long-arm was the Model 1728 *fusil*; this was an improvement on the first standard musket, issued from 1717, and was further modified by the introduction of metal ramrods to replace wooden ones from 1741 onwards. A significant feature was that the barrel was held in place by three metal bands, making it easier to strip down and clean. The

---

1    Stack to M. Delpeck, 24 January 1746, quoted in Christopher Duffy, *The '45. Bonnie Prince Charlie and the Untold Story of the Jacobite Rising* (London: Cassel, 2003), pp.88-89.

calibre was 0.69 inches, somewhat smaller than the contemporary British equivalent. A leather sling was fitted to the side of the musket, rather than underneath as with most similar weapons.

The musket was fitted to take a socket bayonet, which was carried in a leather scabbard when not in use. This was a fairly crude weapon with only a two-step mortice to hold it in place rather than a full zig-zag locking arrangement, and had a 14-inch triangular blade. Also carried with the bayonet on the soldier's waist-belt was a sword – a straight-bladed *epée* or hanger with a double-edged blade for fusiliers, and a heavier single-edged curved sabre for grenadiers.

The waist-belt supporting these two weapons was of buff leather, as were the straps of the two other major items carried by a soldier on campaign. The first of these was the cartridge box or *giberne*, worn on the right hip with the strap over the left shoulder. The box itself was of either reddish-brown or black leather and contained a wooden block drilled out to hold 19 cartridges as well as a small pocket containing tools for the care of the musket. A powder flask, to carry extra powder for re-priming or other emergency use, was suspended from the strap of the *giberne*. Older patterns of cartridge box, fitted to the waist-belt, were no longer in use with regular French troops but were amongst the surplus items supplied for the use of Jacobite forces.

The other major item carried by the soldier was the *havresac*, worn on a single strap over the right shoulder. The bag itself was of heavy linen canvas, and when emptied was big enough to be used as a sort of sleeping bag, covering the lower legs up to the thighs (which would have allowed plenty of overlap with the long shirts of the day). Personal effects and valuables were carried in a cowhide *petit sac* inside the main bag. No standard water canteen was issued, and soldiers were obliged to supply their own – glass or leathern bottles, gourds, or captured enemy equipment are all possibilities here.

In addition to these personal items, soldiers were required to take their turn in carrying items of equipment for general use – hatchets, axes, and other tools; tent poles or canvases; and cooking pots.

Junior NCOs were armed and equipped in the same manner as the ordinary fusiliers and grenadiers. *Sergents*, however, did not carry a musket and *giberne* but were instead issued with a partisan – in French, *pertuisan* – a polearm with a spiked metal blade. This was primarily a badge of rank rather than a fighting weapon, although it was of great use for dressing the ranks, and *sergents* were also issued with an epée of rather better quality than those given to the men in the ranks.

In theory, officers of the rank of *lieutenant* and below had been required since 1710 to arm themselves with a fusil and bayonet, but there seems to be little evidence that this order was actually complied with other than by officers of grenadier companies who typically also carried a cartridge box of the older pattern, fastened to the waist-belt – as private-purchase items, these were rather more ornate than the issue *gibernes* of ordinary soldiers. Field officers, and *capitaines* of fusilier companies, carried a spontoon with a leaf-shaped blade. Naturally, as gentlemen, all officers carried a sword.

## Uniform Details – Irish Picquets

Although men from only four of the Irish regiments actually made it ashore in Scotland, detachments of all six made the attempt to do so and so the uniforms of the whole brigade are discussed here. The base colour of the *justaucorps* was, famously, red for all Irish regiments, this being a madder dye of similar hue to that employed by the British Army. Indeed, it is quite possible in 1745-'46 that the hues were identical, since cloth taken from the captured British depot at Ghent in the aftermath of Fontenoy was subsequently issued to the Irish regiments on the orders of de Saxe.[2]

Since only detachments were sent to Scotland, no regimental colours were sent with them and so need not concern us in this work.

Regimental details were as follows:

Régiment de Bulkeley: this unit furnished only a single picquet for the original contingent, which was amongst those captured at sea. A handful of officers did serve in Scotland, however. Red *justaucorps*, dark green lining, collar, and cuffs; horizontal pockets with three buttons. During the earlier part of the century, the *justaucorps* buttonholes had been laced; by 1741, this had been replaced by white stitching around the buttonholes. Dark green waistcoat and breeches; silver hat lace, pewter buttons.

Régiment de Clare: this unit provided one picquet for the original contingent, which was amongst those captured at sea. The remainder of the regiment sailed from Dunkirk in spring 1746 but was unable to land. Red *justaucorps*; yellow lining and cuffs (no collar); horizontal pockets with three buttons. Yellow waistcoat and breeches, silver hat lace, pewter buttons. The Gudenus manuscript shows an unusual cuff of 'mitre' pattern rising to a point near the elbow where it was held by a single button: it is unclear whether this style was still being worn in 1745.

Régiment de Dillon: this unit provided one picquet for the original contingent, which successfully landed in Scotland. Red *justaucorps*; white lining; black cuffs; horizontal pockets with three buttons. White waistcoat and breeches, gold hat lace, brass buttons. The Gudenus manuscript, whilst depicting the uniform described, shows, or at least hints at, two other details. The first of these is a black collar of an unusual pattern known as an *étole* (stole), with long ends hanging loose down the front of the coat. This style was fashionable in the 1730s but was going out of use; by 1745 it is unclear if it was still being worn, had been replaced with a conventional collar of the same colour, or dispensed with completely. Some sources indicate that a red collar was being worn by the late 1740s, which further complicates things, although black collars were back by 1753. Regulations, at least, would tend towards no collar in 1745. The second detail shown by Gudenus is red lacing on the waistcoat, along with multiple rows of buttons: unfortunately, exactly how this worked is unclear. The lowest button is shown fastened and seems to be flanked by a dummy button to either side, linked to it by red lace; the remaining rows show only the two flanking buttons and not the central one,

---

2    O'Conor, *Military History of the Irish Nation*, p.399.

although this may simply indicate that Gudenus' model had not fastened these buttons. In that no official mention is ever made of this lacing and extra buttons, and that such decoration had been prohibited by the *ordonnance* of 1736, it seems most likely that by 1745 the waistcoat was plain white with no embellishments.

Régiment de Rooth: this unit provided one picquet for the original contingent, which successfully landed in Scotland. Red *justaucorps*; dark blue lining and cuffs (no collar); horizontal pockets with three buttons. Dark blue waistcoat and breeches, gold hat lace, brass buttons.

Régiment de Berwick: this unit provided one picquet for the original contingent, which was amongst those captured at sea. The remainder of the regiment sailed with Clare's, but was likewise unable to land, apart from a single picquet that joined the army before Culloden. Yet another picquet accompanied the gold shipment aboard the *Prince Charles* and was lost with it. Red *justaucorps*; white lining and cuffs (no collar); horizontal pockets with three buttons. White waistcoat and breeches, silver hat lace, pewter buttons.

Régiment de Lally: this unit provided one picquet for the original contingent, which successfully landed in Scotland. Red *justaucorps*; green lining, cuffs, and collar; horizontal pockets with three buttons. Green waistcoat, white breeches; gold hat lace, brass buttons.

Drummers of all six regiments wore the liveries of their colonels and the exact combinations are not always known, or clear. For the Régiment de Dillon, the family colours were red and black and a later depiction indicates red *justaucorps*, with black cuffs and no collar, extensively decorated with double lines of lace in a white and red chevron pattern, worn with red breeches and waistcoat. For the Régiment de Berwick, the Stuart colours of yellow with red appear to have been adopted, with white lace; which elements were red and which yellow is unclear. Drums were decorated with the colonel's coat of arms: the base colour for the Régiment de Dillon is shown as being red but base colours for the other regiments are open to conjecture. There was no official place in the French army at this time for fifers, although accounts suggest that the regiments of the Irish Brigade did have them and that their attack at Fontenoy was accompanied by the strains of 'The White Cockade'. Assuming that this is correct, such men would most likely have been carried on the rolls as ordinary soldiers; whether they wore drummer's livery, and whether any of them accompanied the detachments sent to Scotland, are both unknown.

## Uniform Details – Régiment Royal Ecossois

Of all the French forces employed in this campaign, the one that generates the greatest amount of confusion over their dress is the Royal Ecossois. Successive authors have misinterpreted or taken out of context the information that we have about the regiment, further confusing matters by incorporating details that postdate the events of 1745. As each has taken from another, one man's speculation has become another man's facts until an entirely distorted picture of the regiment's appearance has come into being. We need, therefore, to return first of all to the basic core uniform prescribed for this unit and worn, insofar as we can be certain of any uniform details from a 200-odd year remove, by the majority of its officers and men. Only with that in place can we then look at the various alternative interpretations and unofficial or semi-official alterations. The majority of these can be grounded in fact and do have their place in the story, but that place is a far less significant one than many publications would have us believe.

Blue *justaucorps*; red lining (no collar); horizontal pockets with three buttons. Cuffs were red, with a blue cuff flap and three buttons, and the buttonholes down the front of the *justaucorps* were picked out with white mohair stitching: this latter point has been misinterpreted to imply that the coats were actually laced, in the fashion of the French foot guards regiments, but this is erroneous. Red waistcoats and breeches, silver hat lace, pewter buttons. The buttonholes of the waistcoat were picked out with decorative stitching in the same manner as those of the *justaucorps*.

As a royal regiment, the drummers wore the royal livery; a blue *justaucorps* with red lining and cuffs, decorated with crimson lace picked out with a white chain. Breeches and waistcoat were red. The drums bore the crowned arms of France on a blue background. The regiment was accompanied by at least one piper, but just as there was no official place for fifers at this time, so too were pipers an unofficial extra. Most likely these men were in the private employ of the officers, in the same manner as civilian musicians in regimental bands, and were not bound by uniform regulations: it would therefore seem logical that they wore traditional highland dress. They were also evidently men of some stature; no piper is recorded amongst the regiment's prisoners, but John McDougal is listed as 'Piper's Servant'.[3]

Since the entire regiment was sent to Scotland, it took its regimental colours with it. It is unlikely that these were carried on the field at Inverurie or Falkirk, where only detachments were present, but they were certainly carried at Culloden. The regimental colour – the *drapeau d'ordonnance* – had as its base the Scottish saltire, white on a blue ground, decorated with large heraldic thistles in the centre surrounding a gold *fleur de lys* and with smaller *fleurs de lys* decorating the arms of the cross. The colonel's colour had the identical design, but on a plain white ground. The Latin motto 'Nemo me impune lacessit' (roughly, 'no-one can harm me unpunished', the ancient motto of the Stuart dynasty) was carried in a white scroll at the top of the field. As was the norm for all French regiments, a white cravat was tied around the head of the flagpole, just below the finial.

Certain of these details are specific to the initial incarnation of the regiment during the 1740s, and had changed by the time that the reorganised regiment took part in the campaigns of the Seven Years War a decade later. In that this era is generally better-documented, some reconstructions of the regimental dress have drawn on aspects from this later era. In particular, white eventually replaced red for the breeches and for the coat lining, but

---

3    Livingstone of Bachuil, et al. (eds.) *Muster Roll*, p.62.

this change postdates the events that we are concerned with here. It is also from this later era that another potential red herring originates, which is the wearing of Highland dress by the regiment's grenadier company. The source for this comes from two mentions in reports from the early 1750s detailing the dress of French regiments. The first, from the *2e Carte Militaire ou Liste Générale des Troupes de France* of 1754 simply says '*Les Grenadiers sans Culottes*', that is to say, 'the Grenadiers [are] without breeches': this should surely be taken as meaning that they were wearing something else to cover their modesty, rather than parading in their shirt-tails, which leads to the obvious conclusion that a belted plaid was being worn. This is confirmed by the second mention, from four years later in *Ettrenes Militaries*, which more explicitly states '*La Compagnie des Grenadiers est habillée à la Montagnarde Ecossoise*', that is to say, 'The Grenadier Company is dressed in the fashion of Scots Highlanders'. This is fairly conclusive, but it does not necessarily mean that this clothing was widely worn. Considering the field-day that French print-makers and caricaturists of a later generation had with depictions of Highlanders in the occupying British army of 1815, it is unlikely that their *ancien régime* counterparts would have restrained themselves had such a dress been worn on a daily basis, but no such images exist. Very likely, then, this highland dress was something worn for the sort of peacetime inspection parades where it was recorded in 1754 and 1758, rather than in the field. More importantly for our purposes, though, the first mention is also almost a decade too late. There is not one mention of Highland dress being worn by the regiment before 1754, and only these two official mentions to indicate its use after this date. Considering the relatively low proportion of Scots – and, by extrapolation from that, the even lower proportion of true Highlanders – in the rank and file of the regiment before 1745, this is hardly surprising.

If these diversions from the standard uniform can safely be dismissed as postdating our era, however, there are two other points that require our more detailed consideration because the one stems from a contemporary account and the other relates to a surviving artefact. In both cases, however, the significance of the points in question has been taken out of context, and extrapolations made from them that have led to considerable distortions of their relevance.

The first of these points relates to the idea that the regiment adopted a uniform of short coats and blue Scots bonnets either prior to, or during, its deployment to Scotland. Certainly we do have a source for this, an account of the trial of *Lieutenant* Charles Oliphant, in which one Andrew Robertson testified as follows:

> I saw the prisoner with the rebels at Fochabers and Elgin in Moray when the rebel army, and particularly Lord John Murray's regiment, lay there, and were in possession of those places, and the prisoner wore the uniform of Lord John Drummond's officers, viz: – short blue coats, red vests laced, with bonnets and white cockades.[4]

---

4    Allardyce (ed.), *Historical Papers Relating to the Jacobite Period*, Vol.2, p.402.

How typical Oliphant's attire was is, however, open to question, for he was not one of the officers who accompanied the regiment over from France but, rather – as we have seen – a locally-recruited addition. Presumably, then, such uniform as he was able to assemble was composed of items borrowed from, or donated by, his new fellow officers, along with such as could be made up locally which no doubt goes some way to explaining the (apparently plain) short coat worn instead of the *justaucorps*.

That said, Robertson's testimony does state that the clothing worn by Oliphant was 'the uniform of Lord John Drummond's officers', implying that such a 'dressed-down' attire was not unique to the former excise man, and, indeed, an account of Drummond himself suggests that he also affected a similar outfit, albeit definitely with lacing on the short-coat. The crucial word in the Robertson testimony, however, is *officers*. As we have seen, the majority of the regiment's officer corps were Scots and, considering how difficult it was to get French army officers of any nationality to wear their regulation uniforms when on duty – necessitating in 1729 the issue of a royal order to insist on it – it is hardly surprising that at least some of them made adaptations to their dress so as to reflect their own preferences and national character. In Drummond's case, too, it should be noted that for the bulk of the Rising he was not serving with his regiment but acting as a Jacobite general officer and, as we have seen, officers so detached from their parent regiments tended not to wear their regular uniforms anyway.

Neither Oliphant nor Drummond is therefore a typical example of a Royal Ecossois officer during the '45, so much so that it is unrewarding to extrapolate from their example to second-guess how the officers who served with the battalion might have dressed. Either way, and in contrast to the assumptions made by a number of authors, there are no contemporary mentions of any alterations to dress being made by the regiment's rank and file. Officers' uniforms, as outlined by the same royal edict that made wearing them on duty compulsory, were privately purchased by the officers: conversely, soldiers' uniforms were issued on a three-yearly cycle and so mass alterations of the sort implied by writers who assume that the men were dressed in the same manner as is described for Oliphant and Drummond would hardly have been viable from a financial point of view. With this in mind, and in the absence of any evidence to the contrary relating to the dress of non-commissioned members of the regiment either during their time in Scotland or in Flanders prior to their being embarked, it should therefore be taken as a given that the rank and file were dressed in accordance with regulations.

The second point to address is the wearing of British-style 'mitre' grenadier caps. A cap exists, now in the National Museum of Scotland, which was once listed as having belonged to Charles Edward Stuart but which is now understood to have belonged to an officer of the Royal Ecossois. The cap is an undeniably beautiful item, the stiffened blue velvet front decorated with a large embroidered Star of the Order of the Thistle and the silver-laced false peak with a fleur de lys flanked by sprays of thistles. The latter motif also appears on the rear of the cap, whilst the rear bag is red silk.

The provenance of this cap is discussed at length in an article by Stephen Wood in the *Journal of the Society for Army Historical Research*, who notes that the erroneous suggestion that the cap was intended for the Prince stems from a misinterpretation of a piece of decorative work around the stems of the embroidered thistles as a C.S. cypher. It has to be said that one has to squint very hard to see this as anything other than decorative, and Wood rightly dismisses this as a red herring. So too may be dismissed the suggestions that this is a cap from a Scots militia regiment or from a unit in the Scots Brigade in Dutch service; the provenance is tracked by Wood and there seems little doubt but that the cap was indeed amongst the personal effects of one of the passengers aboard the French privateer *Espérance* captured in November 1745 by the *Sheerness* off the Dogger Bank. It soon passed into the hands of the collector Sir Peter Thompson and Wood goes on to speculate that it was purchased by him from one of the captive French officers confined in the Marshalsea Prison awaiting exchange. Wood further suggests that the spurious connection with Prince Charles, in which Thompson evidently believed, may have been introduced by the vendor at this stage to make the item more desirable, the fee accordingly higher, and his incarceration commensurately more comfortable once Thompson had paid up.[5]

French grenadiers of the 1740s wore cocked hats of the same sort as fusiliers, and, when grenadier caps were later adopted these were bearskins rather than of the 'mitre' pattern. This should therefore immediately raise a question over the status of this cap as a regulation item. To set against that, however, caps of a not dissimilar pattern were briefly experimented with by the Gardes Francaises in the 1730s and are shown in the Gudenus Manuscript as being worn by the free-company of Kleinholtz so they were not entirely alien to the French service. However, it is when we extrapolate from the existence of one cap to the idea that such caps were worn more widely that we begin to encounter problems. Although there were five officers of the Royal Ecossois aboard the *Espérance* – *Capitaines* Baillie and Macdonald and *Lieutenants* Nairn, Cameron, and Urquhart – none of these men appear from their service histories to have belonged to the regimental grenadier company, which, indeed, arrived safely in Scotland intact and served through to Culloden. Whilst it is possible that the cap was the property of one of the grenadier officers and being transported for him – perhaps a late delivery from the milliner – this cannot be proven and so there is no direct link to confirm that it represents the headgear of the officers of that company. It then becomes an even bigger leap of faith to suggest that similar caps – for with its velvet, silk, and silver lace this is clearly a private purchase item – were worn by the rank and file of the grenadier company. When we also consider that there is no written mention of such caps being worn by anyone of any rank in Scotland or afterwards, it is safe to say that the reason for this is that they were not. What seems most likely is that this item represents a piece of finery adopted to cut a dash by an officer with funds to spare – perhaps an accessory to be sported as part of the regiment's hoped-for recruiting drive after its

---

5   Stephen Wood, 'An Officer's Mitre Cap of *Le Regiment Royal-Ecossois*, 1745', *JSAHR*, Vol. LXXV No.302 (Summer 1997), pp.77-83.

arrival in Scotland – and was never intended for campaign wear. Exquisite though it is, it adds nothing to our knowledge of the appearance of the men of the Royal Ecossois who actually made it ashore to serve in Scotland.

### Uniform Details – Artillery and Engineers

Moving on to the small contingent of specialist troops who accompanied the French expedition to Scotland we are, thankfully, back on rather more solid ground insofar as uniform details are concerned.

The uniform of the artillery was, as noted, cut in the same fashion as the infantry. The *justaucorps* was dark blue with red lining and cuffs, pockets were horizontal and had five buttons. Brass buttons; gold hat lace. Waistcoats and breeches were also red and were the preferred order of dress when the guns were being served in action, the *justaucorps* being dispensed with. *Sergents* wore the same rank distinctions as their infantry counterparts but carried halberds rather than the infantry *pertuisan*; officers wore the same colour combination as the rank and file but, again like their infantry counterparts, were distinguished by the better quality of the cloth, by gold lacing on the waistcoat, and by the wearing of the gorget when on duty.

Artillery gun carriages were painted red, with the ironwork picked out in black. It may be inferred that guns supplied by the French to the Jacobites also followed this scheme.

French artillery officers c.1745. (The New York Public Library Digital Collections)

The corps of engineers was an all-officer body which had only recently been militarised; such of its officers who served in Scotland did so in an advisory capacity, although *Capitaine* de Saussay notably brought up and commanded a 4-pounder cannon at Culloden and kept it in action almost until the end. Uniform for army engineer officers as decreed in February 1744 consisted of a light blue-grey *justaucorps*, waistcoat, and breeches. Cuffs were black, buttons and hat-lace gold. The buttonholes on the *justaucorps* were also laced in gold. A non-contemporary print, part of an 1899 series by Charles Lyall, shows the *justaucorps* as described but with scarlet breeches and waistcoat; this may indicate a carry-over from the pre-1744 uniform, which was all scarlet apart from blue cuffs on the *justaucorps*, but it is unclear what evidence exists to substantiate this interpretation.

## Uniform Details – Régiment de Fitzjames

So far, all the uniforms addressed have followed the same basic pattern. Cavalry uniforms, however, were somewhat different. Since the Régiment de Fitzjames was the only French cavalry unit involved in this campaign, this section will address both the generalities of heavy cavalry uniforms and the specifics of the uniform of this regiment.

The bulk of the French mounted arm of the 1740s was made up of heavy cavalry regiments, although, confusingly, these were still referred to as *cavalerie légère* – light cavalry – as a hangover from the days when it had been necessary to distinguish them from the true armour-wearing heavies of the 16th century.

The main weapon of the troopers of the *cavalerie légère* was a heavy straight-bladed sword with a brass hilt. The blade was 33 inches in length and the sword was worn from a leather waist-belt. It was supplemented by a carbine – the 1733/4 model, which utilised the same lock as the 1728 infantry musket – and a pair of pistols. However, because the men sent to Scotland were dispatched without their horses, the carbines were left behind and the men issued with infantry muskets and bayonets to enable them to better do duty on foot if required; this would have meant that those men who were able to be mounted in Scotland would only have had their swords and pistols.[6] The pistols were carried in a pair of holsters either side of the saddle, and the carbine butt-uppermost on the right-hand side. A carbine belt was worn over the left shoulder, to which the carbine was affixed by a swivel and slider. Ammunition was carried in a small leather cartridge pouch worn on a narrow strap over the right shoulder. Saddle-clothes and holder-covers were of different colours for different regiments; in the case of Fitzjames, these were yellow laced with white.

Like the infantryman's *justaucorps*, the cavalryman's coat was cut long and loose in a slightly dated fashion; however, unlike in the case of the infantry, most

Officer of Engineers c.1745 by Charles Lyall. Lyall here depicts the smallclothes as being scarlet as per the pre-1744 uniform, but the details are otherwise accurate. (Anne S.K. Brown Military Collection)

---

6    The carbines were placed in store, and reclaimed by the regiment when it was re-established after the Rising. See O'Conor, *Military History of the Irish Nation*, p.401.

regiments – Fitzjames included – wore lapels on their coats which, per a regulation of 1733, were to extend down to the waist and no lower. In the case of the Régiment de Fitzjames the coat was the same madder red as the Irish infantry, with cuffs, lining, and lapels in blue and pewter buttons. The pockets were horizontal and had three buttons, and the buttons fastening the coat itself were set in pairs. The black cocked hat was edged with false-silver lace and a metal skull-cap or 'secret' could be worn underneath it for added protection in combat. In cold or wet weather, a loose cape was worn – for the Régiment de Fitzjames this was red. Gloves were worn for parade only.

Standard to all regiments of the *cavalerie légère*, the breeches and waistcoats were made of buff leather for protection against wear and to give them some chance of turning a blow from an edged weapon. They were fastened with brass buttons. Further protection for mounted combat could be afforded by wearing a black iron cuirass (breastplate only), but this was not a popular item and was often not worn – it is certainly unlikely in the extreme that its extra weight could have been borne by the dubious collection of second-hand horseflesh that was employed to mount the squadron that served in Scotland, and it would certainly have been abandoned by those men obliged to fight dismounted. Dismounted troopers would, however, have been obliged to make the best of things in their knee-length black leather boots, as no provision appears to have been made for the issue of shoes and gaiters.

Officer and NCO ranks were indicated in much the same way as in the infantry, with the *maréchaux de logis* wearing metallic lace around the top of their cuffs in the same manner as infantry *sergents*. NCOs were armed in the same way as the troopers, but officers carried only a sword and pistols, these being private-purchase items of good quality.

Trumpeters and kettledrummers wore the livery of the colonel; the Stuart colours of yellow with red, in the form of a yellow coat with red lining. Lacing is unknown – possibly it was white as with the Régiment de Berwick whose drummers also wore the Stuart colours. The trumpet banners bore the arms of Fitzjames – quartered with the lilies of France, leopards of England, lion of Scotland, and Irish harp – most likely on a yellow ground with silver trimming. As noted, the regiment had maintained the practice of having black trumpeters but it is unclear whether this tradition lasted into the 1740s.

## Miscellaneous Troops

The attire of the Compagnie de Maurepas has already been discussed. The uniform of naval officers was not formally regulated until 1751; however, since the reign of Louis XIV a blue coat had been specified, decorated with gold braid, but beyond this there was little uniformity. Ordinary sailors had no official uniform.

The various stray army officers from regiments not covered above would most likely have worn the uniform of their various units. As noted, the standard French infantry uniform was based on a white *justaucorps* but there is not space here to go into the details when many of these units were represented by only a single individual. The chaplain Alexander Gordon as an *aumônier militaire* would have worn standard clerical garb; the surgeons, and the interpreter attached to the Royal Ecossois, would likewise have worn civilian dress. The small number of Spanish officers who also ended up in Scotland, and who are generally lumped in with the French in the various listings of prisoners, came primarily from the Irish regiments of the Spanish army whose red uniforms broadly resembled those of their French equivalents.

# 4

# French Troops in Scotland

## Landing and First Moves

The first of the ships carrying the Royal Ecossois and Irish Picquets sailed from Dunkirk on 26 November (NS) 1745. As we have seen from the study of the men captured in them, the *Louis XV* with the picquets of Bulkeley, Berwick, and Clare aboard, and the *Espérance* with part of the Royal Ecossois, were both intercepted but the remaining ships made it safely to Scottish ports. In this they were helped in no part by a ferocious gale that wrecked two ships of the Royal Navy squadron watching the Scottish coast. Even so, the brand-new 28-gun frigate *La Fine*, with Lord John Drummond on board as well as the expedition's artillery, was chased into Montrose by the British 40-gun *Milford* and ended up running aground in the process whilst the 30-gun *Renommée*, with the bulk of the troops embarked, had a narrow escape from the 50-gun *Newcastle*. The arrival of the French squadron at Montrose was particularly fortuitous for the local Jacobites since they had been until then engaged in a mini-campaign waged against the crew of the British sloop *Hazard*, of 10 guns, whose captain had been attempting to rally the Government sympathisers in the area. Now, with French troops and heavy artillery, the tables were turned and the British ship was swiftly captured, being subsequently equipped as a privateer in French service under the name *Prince Charles*.

Because some of the French ships had landed their cargoes at Peterhead and Stonehaven, it took some time for Drummond's little force to properly assemble itself. He had his own regiment of Royal Ecossois – perhaps 400-strong after allowing for the captures at sea, down from a known effective strength of 28 officers and 487 rank and file in June 1745 – and the surviving half of the Irish Picquets, composed of the detachments of Dillon, Rooth, and Lally, with in the region of another 170 all ranks.[1] There was also an artillery detachment with six guns – two 16-pounders, two 12-pounders, and two 8-pounders – manned by the only truly French element of the force. Landed on 24 November, these would represent the heaviest ordnance in

---

1    June figure for the Royal Ecossois from Colin, *Campagnes de Maréchal de Saxe*, Vol.III, p.482.

the Jacobite arsenal during the whole of the Rising, and were backed up by a half-dozen 6-pounders taken from the captured *Hazard* which were made available to the local Jacobites.

The arrival of the French forces also allowed Drummond the excuse for some political manoeuvring designed to sway the balance of power in Britain to a far greater extent than merely the arrival of a few hundred French troops would achieve. During the response to the initial news of the Rising, it was not just British troops who were brought over from the Continent but nine battalions of Dutch troops also. These came from the garrison of Tournai, which had surrendered to the French after Fontenoy; the men had been released on parole not to fight against the French but nobody had said anything about the Jacobites and so the Dutch were shipped over to join Marshal Wade's army which operated on the eastern side of the Pennines during the English campaign. Now, Drummond sent word that with his troops in the field the Jacobites were acting as auxiliaries of the French and thus the Dutch

Lord John Drummond, oil on canvas by Domenico Duprà. (Public Domain)

would be in breach of their parole if they continued to serve in the British Isles; they were therefore obliged to return to the Continent, and although Hessian troops were engaged in their place these would take some time to arrive and would play only a limited role in the closing stages of the Rising. Independently of Drummond's initiative, the French officers at Carlisle made a similar protest when it was reported that Wade had sent some of the Dutch troops over the hills to reinforce Cumberland's besieging army. In fact, there were only a few Dutch gunners outside Carlisle but Cumberland nevertheless sent them back to Wade – albeit with considerable ill-grace.

Drummond's French rank notwithstanding, he held a Jacobite commission as a lieutenant general which upon his arrival in Scotland made him the senior Jacobite officer there in place of Viscount Strathallan. Active command of the French troops therefore devolved onto *Lieutenant-Colonel* Walter Stapleton of the Régiment de Berwick, acting as a *brigadier des armées du roi*. This rank – literally, brigadier of the King's armies, to distinguish it from the cavalry non-commissioned rank of *brigadier* although the short form was generally employed in all but the most formal of circumstances – existed to allow regimental officers to exercise brigade command during wartime, and was typically conferred for good service; in Stapleton's case, after the Battle of Fontenoy. Little seems to be known about Stapleton; even O'Callaghan's dense 1885 history of the Irish Brigade, usually replete with genealogical information and dubious pedigrees, notes only that he came from an old Munster family. He was clearly – as evidenced by his promotion after Fontenoy – a brave and competent officer and, insofar as he appears in accounts of the campaign in anything other than a formal military role, the impression that one gets is of a reserved and honourable gentleman.

Whilst all eyes were turned to Charles' invasion of England, the war in Scotland was by no means over. Arriving on the eastern coast of Scotland, Drummond was able to link up with the Jacobite forces being raised in that area, primarily under the aegis of Lord Lewis Gordon. Younger brother of the Duke of Gordon, Lord Lewis was a former Royal Navy lieutenant but had sided with the Jacobites after Prestonpans and been sent back to the Gordon lands around Banff and Aberdeen with orders to raise troops. He eventually assembled a regiment of three battalions: James Moir of Stoneywood's, raised largely in and around Aberdeen and containing mostly genuine volunteers, Francis Farquharson of Monaltrie's, raised largely in Braemar and Deeside, and John Gordon of Avochie's, raised in Strathbogie. These last two, and Avochie's in particular, contained a sizeable proportion of pressed men and suffered from desertion. Also raised in the area were weak battalions – little more than overstrength companies – raised by James Crichton of Auchingoul around Aberdeen and by Sir Alexander Bannerman of Elsick around Stonehaven. More successful in his recruiting efforts than these two was Sir James Kinloch, sent into Forfarshire to form a second battalion for Lord Ogilvie's Regiment. Kinloch was able to raise some 300 men, who would become some of the best-drilled and most effective of all the Jacobite infantry, in no small part down to the fact that he acquired the services of *Lieutenant* Nicolas Glascoe of the Regiment de Dillon who was seconded to assist him as the battalion's major. Like Bagot with the hussars, Glascoe was another French officer who made a significant impact on the Jacobite army in a training and leadership role, but the regiment that he joined would end up having a far stronger connection to the French service than any of the other units and it is therefore worth digressing for a moment to look at it, its commander, and Glascoe, in more detail.

David, Lord Ogilvie, was the son and heir of the 5th Earl of Airlie, and came from a family with a long history of devoted service to the House of Stuart. The 5th Earl managed to sit on the fence in 1745, but his late brother, the 4th Earl, had been active in the '15 and he was apparently quite content for his 20-year-old heir to raise the tenants of the family's Forfarshire estates to form the initial 600-man regiment that joined the Jacobite army after Prestonpans and took part in the English campaign. Meanwhile, as noted, Kinloch was sent to raise a second battalion and the combined regiment is estimated to have fielded as many as 900 men at Falkirk and was still 500-strong at Culloden. As well as being a charismatic leader, Ogilvie sought to instil a far greater degree of professionalism, uniform, and discipline than was the Jacobite norm into his command, which was, for example, one of a handful of Jacobite regiments to boast a grenadier company. He had already acquired a modicum of professional experience notwithstanding his youth, having travelled to France in late 1743 to attend the *Ecole Militaire* in Paris (this was after studying at the University of Aberdeen and carrying out an elopement and clandestine marriage at the age of 16 – truly, his was an eventful life). Ogilvie was listed as an *officier reformé* in the Royal Ecossois with the rank of *capitaine* as of 1 August 1744, but, as with many of the leading Jacobites commissioned into the regiment this seems to have been by way of a holding position pending the launching of the Rising; certainly, by the time of the '45, the young nobleman was back in Scotland.

The appointment of *Lieutenant* Glascoe to the staff of Kinloch's battalion meant that both elements of the regiment possessed someone with prior military experience, but in passing it should be noted that Glascoe's appointment as major perhaps owed more to the French conception of the rank – a sort of second-in-command-cum-adjutant – than the simple subordinate role implied by the English-language usage. Certainly he seems to have exercised a considerable degree of influence within the regiment, even after the two battalions were united under Ogilvie's personal command. It has further been suggested that Ogilvie's Regiment was counted as one – or perhaps both, if the two battalions are counted as individual units – of the two regiments of Scottish infantry that Louis XV authorised on 15 February (NS) 1746 in response to a suggestion that some of the troops being raised in Scotland be taken directly into French pay. This initiative seems to have replaced the abortive plan to raise an additional battalion for the Royal Ecossois, but came too late to have any real effect on matters during the Rising. The argument for Ogilvie's Regiment being taken into French pay is made by Helen McCorry in her study of the Scots regiments in French service,[2] but no concrete evidence is provided and it is odd that none of the officers of the regiment who fell into Government hands after Culloden employed their putative French commissions as part of their defence in the way that Glascoe – who undoubtedly was a bona fide French officer – did. Most likely, this scheme was overtaken by events.

The French connection of Lord Ogilvie's Regiment aside, it may be wondered why so much ink has been spilled describing the rag-tag of Jacobite forces that Drummond found at his disposal on arriving in Scotland. The answer is that they would form the supporting cast in the first significant occasion to see French troops in action on Scottish soil, which came at Inverurie on 23 December 1745. Coming after Prestonpans, Falkirk, and Culloden in the order of things, this was one of the largest of the small battles of the '45, yet is generally little known. It shows, however, just how effective French troops and French officers were when it came to providing stiffening to their Jacobite allies and, as Christopher Duffy has wryly pointed out, completely inverts the popular conception of the '45 by pitting Lowlanders and regulars fighting for the Stuarts against Highlanders fighting for George II.

At the time of Drummond's arrival in Scotland, the main Jacobite army was still in England, although by the time he had his forces assembled it had already begun to retreat. It is, therefore, difficult to see how Drummond could have materially aided the English campaign at so late a juncture. In any case, he elected not to do so – citing logistical difficulties, which, with his artillery train was a not-unreasonable point – and instead set about consolidating Jacobite control over Scotland by concentrating his forces – French and Jacobite – around Perth with a view to reducing the strongholds of Stirling and Edinburgh Castles. This, however, meant abandoning operations further

---

2    McCorry, 'Rats, Lice and Scotsmen', pp.22-23

north where there was an ongoing struggle within the Highlands between the pro-Stuart and pro-Hannover clans. Colonel John Campbell, Earl of Loudoun, commanded the Government forces in the Highlands, but aside from the static garrisons his force also consisted of local levies built onto a core of detachments from the British Army's two Highland regiments; Murray's 43rd and Loudoun's own 64th. Clans loyal to George II included the MacLeods, Munros, and Grants, who provided much of the manpower for the 18 Independent Companies of Highlanders authorised by Loudon. As with the clans that came out for Charles, this is not to say that the clan itself made the choice, but rather that the chief did: this, in turn, could be down to a variety of factors, not least of which was the chance to settle old scores with rivals who had backed the other side.

By December 1745, Loudoun reckoned that he had sufficient manpower to crush Gordon: he was, as yet, unaware that Drummond's French reinforcements had arrived. However, the decision of Lord Lovat to bring Clan Fraser out for the Stuarts distracted his attention and, believing this to be the major threat, Loudoun set off with all his regulars and half of the new Independent Companies to crush Lovat.

In his absence, Norman MacLeod of MacLeod was sent with five Independent Companies, four of them drawn from his own clan militia, to keep an eye on the Jacobite forces at Aberdeen. Later, deciding that this was too small a force, Loudoun sent two more companies. MacLeod might also have had the aid of the Clan Grant militia, whose laird, Ludovick Grant of Grant, had put 400 men into the field for the Government only to be told by Loudoun that they could neither be paid nor armed and must thus be disbanded. Grant promptly sent his men home, although their brief appearance in the field had caused the Jacobites to abandon Fochabers, controlling the passage of the Spey, and retire on Aberdeen. With his path accordingly cleared, MacLeod marched his outnumbered command into Jacobite territory, reaching Oldmeldrum on 20 December. There, they at last received news that the French had landed, and the ill-fated decision was taken to put the force into billets in and around the small town of Inverurie, 15 miles from Aberdeen, to await the arrival of Loudoun with reinforcements.

Whilst MacLeod busied himself securing the best billets in Inverurie for his own clansmen, posting the other three companies in farms and hamlets to the north, Lord Lewis Gordon had preparations well under way to disturb his rest. Drummond had taken most of his French troops down to Perth, but left two companies of the *Royal Ecossois* to help hold Aberdeen, under the command of *Major* Lachlan Cuthbert, with whose aid Lord Lewis was able to form a plan to march on Inverurie.

On the morning of 23 December, therefore, 1,200 men left Aberdeen to begin the attack. The Jacobite plan called for an approach in two columns, one of which would attack directly from the south while the other, larger, force would come in from the east. Cuthbert commanded the larger column, which included the French regulars and was accompanied by Lord Lewis in person although he left the command to Cuthbert, whilst the smaller was under Major Jean Gordon and consisted of Kinloch's battalion of Ogilvie's Regiment and the battalion of John Gordon of Avochie. Because this column had a shorter distance to travel, over easier terrain, it arrived in the vicinity of Inverurie before the main force: accordingly, Gordon ordered a halt at Kinellar, six miles to the south, and sent scouts forward in order to have news of his allies and his enemies. Unbelievably, MacLeod had not seen fit to post any sentries, and neither the Jacobite scouts nor their main body were spotted. The main column also approached Inverurie without detection, but having also arrived early several of the undisciplined Jacobites broke ranks to get a closer look at their objective and this at last ensured that the alarm was raised, late in the afternoon.

Inverurie lies between the waters of the Don and Urie, which join just below the town: in order to attack, Gordon's column would have to cross the former and Cuthbert's the latter, and there were only two fords. In theory at least, the defenders could hold one ford with a skeleton force, enabling them to concentrate against the other attack and defeat the Jacobites in detail. In the event, however, neither MacLeod nor his men were up to the task. Indeed, from the outset MacLeod seems to have assumed that he was beaten, in particular once it became clear that his attackers included the regulars of the Royal Ecossois. These two companies led the attack of Cuthbert's column, moving quickly towards the Urie ford. This was situated next to the remains of an ancient castle, whose motte – known as The Bass – entirely dominated the crossing, but MacLeod abandoned both ford and motte without a fight to take up a position nearer the town. Thus, Cuthbert was able to get his whole force across and form a line of battle, with the regulars taking the post of honour on the right, facing off against the 400 or so MacLeods defending the town. Unaccountably, no attempt was made to call in the three outlying companies, whose arrival would have given MacLeod parity with Cuthbert's forces. For a time, the Government Highlanders stood their ground and kept up a good fire: indeed, they performed better than the pressed men of Lord Lewis Gordon's battalions, who began to falter almost from the start.

Only the disciplined fire of the French regulars sustained the battle for the Jacobites, but help was at hand as *Major* Gordon's column was seen approaching the Don ford on the flank of the Government line. MacLeod now ordered a retreat, and his men fell back into Inverurie itself. The town consisted, apart from a few outlying buildings, of a single long street which the regulars of the *Royal Ecossois* now cleared by methodical street-firing, moving forwards a section at a time. It is telling, considering that there is a tendency to credit French infantry of this era with a fairly basic tactical repertoire, that accounts specify that the two companies delivered a disciplined fire throughout the action and that the street-firing was successfully maintained without degenerating into the more common running fire when each man loaded as soon as he was ready.

Driven from the town, and now outnumbered three to one, the surviving Macleods broke and fell back, making their escape to the north into the darkness along with the three outlying companies, none of which had been engaged. Inverurie was hardly a bloodbath: five dead on the Government side and two more mortally wounded, as against nine dead Jacobites most of them from the Royal Ecossois. Total wounded on both sides came to around 20 men, but, more significantly, the Jacobites took 60 prisoners and this, and the flight of their opponents, enabled them to claim the victory. Nevertheless, the MacLeods fought well – more like regulars than militia, according to Cuthbert – whilst most of the Jacobites scarcely fought at all: only 60 or so men of Gordon's column followed him across the Don, whilst in Cuthbert's column nearly all the fighting was done by the regulars. The end result, however, was that Aberdeen was secure for the time being. With Loudoun still off on his wild goose chase after the wily Lord Lovat, Gordon and Cuthbert could therefore take their men down to join Drummond at Perth, from where the whole contingent would link up with Prince Charles now that the main Jacobite army was once again on Scottish soil.

### The Campaign of Stirling and Falkirk

The new year of 1746 found the Jacobite army of Prince Charles Edward Stuart in Glasgow, regrouping and re-provisioning after its failed attempt to invade England. Although the decision to turn back at Derby rather than press on to London is generally touted as the turning point of the '45, a return to Scotland allowed Charles to concentrate his forces with those of Drummond and Lord Lewis Gordon and to potentially re-establish a power base north of the border. What was more, the Government forces were scattered and worn out after forced marches in pursuit of the fast-moving Jacobites, leaving Charles with a brief window of opportunity during which the strategic initiative was again in his hands. To set against this, morale in the Jacobite forces was low after the failed campaign in England, with command relations – stormy at the best of times – badly strained. Lack of intelligence further limited Charles' options: indeed, the reason that his men were in Glasgow at all, rather than further south around Dumfries, was because of false rumours that the Duke of Cumberland was moving into Scotland with the army that had taken Carlisle. In fact, Cumberland had returned to London – that, along with an initial unwillingness to send all available forces north, was one of the few tangible benefits of the threatened French invasion – and left Lieutenant General Henry Hawley in command of the Government forces in the field. As Charles regrouped around Glasgow, Hawley assembled his forces around Newcastle and then pushed northwards to occupy Edinburgh, bringing the two sides ever closer to direct confrontation.

In hindsight, it would seem as if Charles' best option would have been to attack Hawley before he could complete the concentration of his army: assuming a Jacobite victory, this would have most likely recovered Edinburgh for the Stuarts. Instead, Charles led his army north with the objective of laying siege to Stirling Castle, continuing the strategy embarked upon by Drummond of securing the southern fortresses and cutting the main Government forces off from the Highlands. On 8 January 1746, the town of Stirling surrendered to the Jacobites, but in the castle the aging Major General Blakeney and his polyglot garrison continued to resist. Blakeney's defiance was not without good reason: Stirling Castle was set high on a volcanic rock, and its medieval walls had been reinforced with embrasures for cannon. This was clearly a job for the heavy guns and specialist officers that Drummond had brought over from France but, against so formidable an obstacle, neither proved to be up to the task.

Indeed, even getting the French contingent there proved to be a time-consuming business, as the march was delayed by the need to move at the pace of the cannon. The men too, would likely have had far more baggage than was the norm for the Scots Jacobite troops, who were known for marching fast and light. Exactly what level of equipment was embarked with Drummond's force is unclear, but the troops assembled for the putative 1745 invasion under Richelieu required 300 wagons to convey all the supplies, munitions, and equipment that was to be embarked for them, which suggests in the region of 14 wagons for each infantry battalion. Even if Drummond's troops were not as encumbered as this, they would certainly have been carrying their tents and a basic supply of food, although no doubt the latter was supplemented by local acquisitions. It would seem, too, that the ranks were already being swelled by local recruits, as it is presumably on the occasion of the French contingent arriving at Stirling that they were joined by one John Denothy, a French wig-maker in the service of the Boyd family of Callendar House.[3]

The French contingent having finally arrived, it was necessary to get the heavy guns brought by Drummond across the Forth and into a position where they could begin to bombard the castle. Against active local opposition, this took time so that no serious work could be undertaken until mid January, by which time Hawley had already begun to push troops north from Edinburgh preparatory to concentrating his army to relieve the siege. On 13 January, Hawley's advance guard under Major General John Huske encountered its Jacobite equivalent – five battalions under Lord George Murray – at Linlithgow, but Murray withdrew without a fight and fell back to Bannockburn. By the 15th, Huske had most of the Government army concentrated at Linlithgow, and on the 16th Hawley assumed command in person and ordered an advance on Falkirk, 10 miles south-east of Stirling, which became his new base of operations. Hawley had some 8,000 men at hand, including over 800 dragoons, but his artillery train was still back in Newcastle and he had only 10 assorted pieces available, with his few regular gunners supplemented by detachments of sailors and raw volunteer infantry of the Yorkshire Blues.

Meanwhile, at Stirling, the Jacobite siege attempts had achieved next to nothing. Accordingly, once it became clear that Hawley was advancing in force the decision was made to leave only a skeleton garrison in the siege lines to guard against a sortie by Blakeney's garrison and to concentrate the remainder of the army for battle. Initial expectations that Hawley would attack the Jacobites at Bannockburn proved unfounded, and so on the morning of 17 January Charles set his forces in motion to attack the Government forces around Falkirk. Hawley's men were encamped on the relatively flat ground immediately to the north of Falkirk, whilst the general

---

3    Geoff B. Bailey, *Falkirk or Paradise! The Battle of Falkirk Muir 17 January 1746* (Edinburgh: John Donald, 1996), p.28.

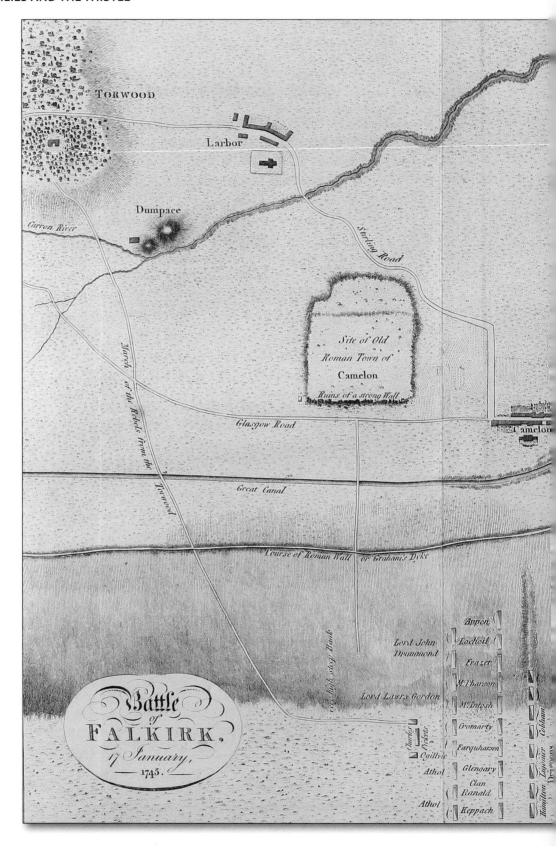

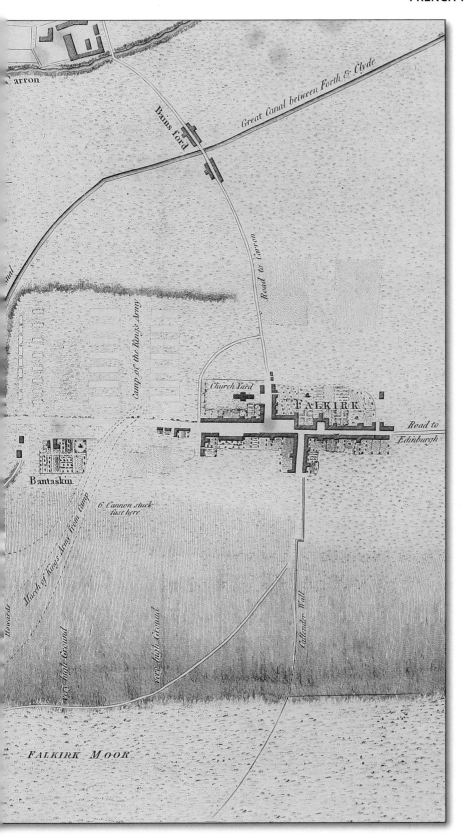

Map of the Falkirk battlefield and environs from John Home's 1802 *The History of the Rebellion in the Year 1745*. As well as showing the field of battle itself, this map also depicts the open terrain to the north where the Jacobite cavalry and French infantry under Lord John Drummond sought to distract the attention of the Government forces away from the main thrust up onto Falkirk Muir.

himself had made his headquarters at Callendar House to the east. Charles elected not to attack directly but rather to make a more circuitous approach that would enable him to seize the high ground of Falkirk Muir to the south of the town. Not only would this ensure that the fight would begin on broken terrain where the Government dragoons would be less formidable, but it also meant that unless Hawley was very quick to react then his troops would be attacking uphill. In order to limit the chances of the Government commander discovering Charles' intentions, a flanking column under Drummond would move ostentatiously towards Falkirk by the direct route before doubling back to re-join the main Jacobite army.

Having been the element of the Jacobite forces most heavily involved in the siege work at Stirling, the bulk of the French contingent could not be spared for the strike against Hawley. All of the artillery was left in place – the lighter pieces as well as the heavy guns – to form part of a covering force under the Duke of Perth tasked with keeping up the blockade of the castle while the main army dealt with Hawley. Only the Irish Picquets were detached to Charles' main army, but, to make up a credible battalion, a fourth picquet was formed from the fusilier companies of the Royal Ecossois whilst the grenadier company of that regiment was attached in its entirety. The end result was a five-company battalion with an all-ranks strength in the region of 275 men, which was commanded by Stapleton in person. Along with the Jacobite cavalry, the battalion took part in Drummond's diversionary sweep. The march, according to a letter written afterwards by an officer of the Royal Ecossois, was marked by atrocious weather – 'rain, hail, and wind' – and it was not until around four o'clock in the afternoon that the battalion took up its position in the Jacobite third line on Falkirk Muir by which time the battle was already underway.[4]

Judging by the evidence, the Jacobites credited Hawley with being rather more vigilant than was actually the case. Despite his superiority in cavalry, there were no patrols or vedettes posted to give advance warning of the enemy, and it was not until early afternoon on the 17 January that Huske received word of the Jacobite advance. Huske immediately began to form the army for battle, but more time was lost as messengers were sent to rouse Hawley from his headquarters and the Jacobites were therefore able to seize the high ground and draw their forces up ready for battle. Charles had a little over 6,100 men under command on Falkirk Muir. Roughly 350 of these were mounted troops and the rest were infantry. The first two lines were composed of the Scots forces, Highland and Lowland, with the right wing under Lord George Murray with the four Clan Macdonald regiments of Keppoch, Clanranald, Glengarry, and Barisdale, supported in the second line by the three battalions of the Athol Brigade. On the left, however, Lord John Drummond was supposed to command but had not yet arrived on the field and there was therefore no effective commander for the first line which comprised a further six clan regiments and one Lowland battalion. Drummond does, at least, seem to have taken charge of the second line

---

4    A.M.D., *Lettre d'un Officier du Regiment Royal Ecossois* (Unknown Publisher, 1746), p.5.

of the left and centre, comprising Ogilvie's Regiment – now united after Ogilvie's own battalion had returned from the English campaign to join Kinloch's which had fought at Inverurie – and of two of Lord Lewis Gordon's battalions. The Jacobite position was anchored on its right by the boggy Glen Burn and on the left by a ravine that extended across the frontage of the leftmost regiments: this latter, however, would prove to be an obstacle when the time came to advance.

Because of the delay in getting news of the advance, and the further delay entailed in getting the information to Hawley's headquarters, it was past three in the afternoon before the Government army began to move up onto the moor; perilously late in the short January day. Leading the way, and therefore ultimately forming the Government left, were the three dragoon regiments brigaded under Colonel Francis Ligonier. Following them were the 12 battalions of regular foot under Huske, assisted by Brigadier Generals James Cholmondley and John Mordaunt, which were under orders to deploy in two lines to the right of the dragoons. In the confusion, the proper brigading was abandoned and the foot deployed in an ad hoc manner, still out of breath after their hurried climb. Far behind the last of the hurrying foot, the Government artillery train was floundering in the mud with its amateur gunners and their escort of Yorkshire volunteers trying and failing to shift the cannon up onto the moor.

With his regular foot so disordered, and his reserves – a mixed Highland battalion and a weak brigade of Glasgow and Paisley volunteers under the Earl of Home – still deploying in the rear, Hawley elected to open the fight with his dragoons. Having fought on the victorious Government right at Sheriffmuir 31 years before, he may well have believed that his 800-odd troopers would chase the Jacobites off the field in a repeat of the same experience. Around four o'clock, with the light already fading fast, the dragoons went forwards against Murray's Jacobites. Being drilled only to a basic level, the Macdonald regiments in Murray's first line were unable to form square to resist the charging horsemen but they fired a volley and then stood their ground to fight it out hand to hand. Accounts suggest that Highland dirks were used to good effect against the bellies of dragoon horses, but, whatever the circumstances, the dragoons soon broke and fell back, a portion of them riding clear off the field and carrying away some of the Earl of Home's volunteer infantry as they did.

Hawley's opening gambit had been a disaster, but both sides seemed equally surprised by the way events had turned out and neither commander was able to act on the changed situation that resulted. The initiative was instead taken by the same Macdonald regiments that had turned back the dragoons. Without orders, they began to pursue the defeated cavalrymen, sweeping over Home's already shaken bluecoats and driving them from the field. Meanwhile, on seeing the Macdonalds go forwards, the remainder of the Jacobite front line spontaneously joined the advance. Prior to the battle, Hawley had done his best to convince his troops that the Highlanders were a rabble who would never stand and fight, but his attempt to boost morale was turned on its head as it became all too apparent to his troops that their commander had got it dead wrong. Except on the far right, where a ravine separated them from the Jacobite far left, the first line of Government foot, not yet recovered from its exertions climbing onto the moor, began to waver before the oncoming Highland charge. To make matters worse for the Government foot, night was now fast coming on, and with it a lashing rain that was blowing directly into their faces. Nevertheless, the bulk of the first line did get off at least one volley before breaking before the assault. As the first line broke, they carried much of the second line with them. Within minutes of the Jacobite charge, the Government left and centre had been swept off the field.

Closest to Falkirk town, on the northern edge of the battlefield, the Government right wing remained substantially intact, protected by the ravine that extended across its front. Aided by Cholmondley, Huske was able to mass four battalions, along with a portion of a fifth and rallied elements of Cobham's and Ligonier's Dragoons, and prepare them for a counter-attack. Having chased the broken Government left and centre, the left flank of the Jacobites was exposed and Huske was able to bring a destructive fire to bear against them with his infantry whilst sending the rallied dragoons against their rear. This caused considerable confusion amongst the Jacobite ranks: even the usually reliable Ogilvie's Regiment wavered for a time, and Glascoe was obliged to rescue one of its colours, dropped by a panicked ensign. It was clear that fresh troops were needed to stabilise the situation.

The only available reserve was Stapleton's little composite French battalion, and it is testament to the difference that they made to the course of the battle that the credit for ordering them into action has been variously attributed to all the heroes of the various factions within the Jacobite high command – O'Sullivan, Murray, and Charles himself. Considering that Murray was off on the right flank, however, O'Sullivan's own account, in which he refers to himself in the third person, seems to have the best ring of truth to it. He records that after witnessing the collapse of the Jacobite left, Charles:

> seeing this brings up the few regular troops he had, rallys six or seven hundred men & orders O'Sullivan to march to a body of horse that was rallied and forming within two musket shots. The horse, seeing this body formed & marching towards them went off as fast as they cou'd drive, as the rest of their Army did, & left us master of the field.[5]

The Jacobite cavalry also moved up at this time, with Lord Elcho's Troop of Lifeguards screening the right flank of the advancing French and the remaining horsemen fanning out further on that flank.

The steady advance of fresh troops at this juncture was enough to put paid to the Government attempt to rally, and as the rearguard of Hawley's army fell back down the slope towards Falkirk town with the French battalion on their heels. Drummond, whose actions prior to this point are hard to place, accompanied them. Charles and Lord George Murray rounded up such of the Scots troops as could be rallied, although it is interesting to note

---

5    John William O'Sullivan (Alistair Tayler and Henriette Tayler eds.), *1745 and After* (London: Thomas Nelson, 1938), pp.118-119.

that O'Sullivan commented with respect to the Scots that little more could be done with troops who were 'so dispers'd and haris'd, by the cruel weather we had, & being under arms all day' but made no such comment with respect to the French battalion which thus became the army's vanguard despite having been all day on the road. O'Sullivan went on to note that:

> Ld John who arrived, had the Van guarde with the Irish picquets & his own, found not a Soul in Falkirk but one Soldier wch he seized upon with his own hands, the souldier struggled with him, got off, fired & shot him in the Arm.[6]

Drummond was not the only French casualty, for the anonymous Royal Ecossois officer who wrote about the battle noted that the regiment had had three officers wounded including Drummond and himself. This officer is identified

Looking down from Falkirk Muir towards the town, modern battlefield monument on the right. (Author's Photo)

only as 'A.M.D.' and described as an *'Ancien Captaine Irlandois'*, which does not immediately match the details of any officer of the regiment. He also fails to specify how and when he was wounded, who the third officer casualty was, or whether there were any rank-and-file casualties (although with three officers hit it has to be inferred that there must have been). He also reports that Drummond had his horse killed under him, which suggests that there was in fact rather more fighting in Falkirk than O'Sullivan's report would suggest, a conclusion shared by the only modern history of the battle.[7]

It being now almost completely dark, the battle was effectively over. However, whilst the Government forces were in no doubt that they had lost, the Jacobites had not yet grasped the nature of their victory, which only became clear at daybreak. Much of the Government artillery train had been secured during the advance on Falkirk, along with baggage including Hawley's own carriage, which was taken by the French battalion as it advanced. Our

---

6   O'Sullivan, p.119.
7   A.M.D., *Lettre*, p.7; see also Bailey, *Falkirk or Paradise!*, pp.147-149.

anonymous officer records plundering by the Scots, but makes no comment either way as to whether or not the French troops joined in, leaving the reader to draw their own conclusions. Prince Charles, it was reported, was able to enjoy the dinner that had been prepared for Hawley. Casualties on both sides were relatively light for so large an action, perhaps in part because the weather was so poor for musketry whilst the Government artillery was never deployed. In the darkness, many troops on both sides had been broken and under such circumstances the length of time taken to appreciate the nature of the Jacobite success can readily be excused; once it had been fully established, however, Charles wasted no time in sending *Capitaine* Browne of the Régiment de Lally, who had re-joined the army after his escape from Carlisle, back to France to present Louis XV with news of the victory. Browne in due course received the cross of the *Ordre de Saint Louis* for his services, before being sent on a new mission to Scotland of which more anon.

In the aftermath of victory, Jacobite hotheads called for a renewed advance on London but cooler heads prevailed and the siege of Stirling Castle, the preparations for which were already underway, was now resumed. In this, a difference quickly emerged between the technical requirements of the siege and the Jacobite requirement to win 'hearts and minds'. Perched high on its hill, the castle had been modified and modernised in the Renaissance to give it some of the features of an artillery fort, and these had been expanded upon in the early 18th century to provide additional outworks on the southern side, facing the town. Grant of the artillery expressed his belief that, notwithstanding these modifications, the only viable means to attack would be from the south where the slope was easiest and even the augmented defences still weaker than those elsewhere. This, however, would place the besieging batteries between the castle and the town of Stirling, so that any 'overs' from the defenders' cannon would damage the town and risk lives, and was accordingly deemed unacceptable. There was, however, an alternative view to set against Grant's, for Drummond had brought over with him a professional officer of engineers, *Chef de Brigade* Francis Mirabelle, who was prepared to offer a different plan.

Lest it be thought that this work is an attempt to demonstrate that the Jacobite army would have been lost without the aid of French professionals, Mirabelle would prove to be something of the evil genius of the siege and the author of a plan that would thwart the Jacobite hopes and cost the lives of many of the French troops engaged in it. Little, however, is known about him. He was, apparently, of Scots ancestry and a number of accounts refer to him as Mirabelle de Gordon; it has even been assumed that Gordon was his surname and Mirabelle a *nom de guerre*, but it is as Mirabell – without the final 'e', although that may simply represent the error of an English clerk – that he appears in a list of French officers confined at Penrith after the Rising, which list also confirms his Christian name and his rank.[8]

Mirabelle's scheme was to open batteries on Gowan Hill, facing the north-eastern front of the castle where there was a defensive battery atop

---

8   'An Etat of the French Officers Prisoners of War att Penrith Ye 11th November 1746', TNA, SP36/89, pp.115-6.

a high cliff. This gave the six attacking guns – only two of which were true siege pieces – 11 defending guns to silence even before they could start battering the walls, and, even if the walls were breached, there was still the cliff to surmount. As if that was not bad enough, the ground on Gowan Hill had little more than a foot of soil before solid rock was reached, which made it extremely difficult to construct trenches, let alone a battery position. Sandbags and woolsacks had to be employed, but, even so, when the first three guns were emplaced and began firing on 30 January, they were all swiftly dismounted by the counter-battery fire from the castle which made clear the utter futility of the scheme. Unsurprisingly, Mirabelle's reputation was soon at rock-bottom, and it was rumoured that a too-great fondness for the bottle was at the root of his poor judgement. James Johnstone wrote that,

Stirling Castle from a 19th century photograph by James Valentine. The far easier approach from the southern aspect (right in the photograph) can be readily appreciated. (The New York Public Library Digital Collections)

> There were formed of him, at first, great hopes of his being able to reduce the castle … believing that an engineer of France of a certain age, and decorated with an order, behoved necessarily to have experience, talents, and capacity, but they discovered, unfortunately too late, that these requisites of his genius were very limited, and that he had not the shadow of judgment, discernment, or good sense; his figure being as ridiculous as his spirits the Highlanders changed his name of Mirabelle, and called him always M. Admirable.[9]

The value of the regular French infantry for siege work, though, was marked. O'Sullivan in his narrative of the campaign recorded:

> The seege continued, & the only hopes we had to succeed was by the Irish picquets & Ld John's Regimt for our does not like to fight against walls, not to work, so there were only these few regular troops – the lowlanders employed at it, our French Ingenier (Mirabel de Gordon) was a headstrong ignorant fellow yt wou'd go his own way & follow no mans advise.[10]

The need to employ the French troops so extensively in so exposed a position, however, meant that casualties amongst them swiftly mounted. Johnstone had much the same to say about the value of the regulars:

---

9    James Johnstone (Trans. Charles Winchester), *Memoirs of the Chevalier de Johnstone* (Aberdeen, D. Wyllie & Son, 1870), Vol.I, p.70.

10   O'Sullivan, *1745 and After*, p.114

Having thus secured the high ground that dominated the fort proper, Grant was able to commence siege operations and a battery was established around 150 yards short of the south-western face of Fort Augustus which began firing the day after the fall of the barracks. From here, saps were driven forwards towards the walls, presumably with the intention of ultimately constructing another mine in order to achieve a breach. This, however, proved to be unnecessary for on 3 March a bomb from one of the Jacobite coehorns smashed through the roof of the fort's powder magazine and set off a devastating explosion. Some accounts suggest that the force of this internal blast was sufficient to breach the wall and render the fort untenable; others suggest that its effects were more significant insofar as their influence on the morale of the garrison was concerned, for the acting-Governor, Major Hu Wentworth, now proposed that the garrison surrender rather than risk the slaughter of an assault. His officers agreed, and terms were concluded on 5 March, Wentworth possibly taking some comfort in the fact that he could at least surrender to regular French officers in the shape of *Brigadier* Stapleton and *Major* Cuthbert rather than to rebellious Highlanders. Some 50 of the garrison were recruited into the ranks of their erstwhile besiegers; although some men had been added after the fall of Fort George, this was the first major infusion of pressganged redcoats into the ranks of the Irish Picquets.

After this success, the force was supposed to have returned to Inverness, but Locheil instead obtained permission to extend the operation and to try and take Fort William as well. This would prove a much tougher nut to crack, having a larger garrison, a substantial stock of artillery, and a resolute Governor in the shape of Captain Caroline Scott. Scott was later a hated scourge of the Jacobites during the post-Culloden pacification of the Highlands and by all accounts something of a nasty piece of work but, undeniably, a first-rate officer. Like Fort Augustus, Fort William was flanked on three sides by water, being built in the angle between Loch Linnhe and the River Nevis. It was overlooked, but the high ground was somewhat further away so that the place was less vulnerable to bombardment. The fort had been under observation by the Jacobites since 24 February, but it took time to move the guns from Fort Augustus and it was not until 15 March that the siege could begin in earnest. Unfortunately, whilst reconnoitring for the best location to begin trench operations, Grant was wounded by a spent shot from one of the fort's swivel guns. The only replacement engineer was Mirabelle, whom Stapleton reluctantly ordered up from Inverness to take over operations: in the meantime, Stapleton sent a formal demand for the garrison to surrender, using the *tambour* of one of the picquets to carry his message which was politely refused by Captain Scott.

Mirabelle, when he arrived, abandoned Grant's plan for sapping forwards and instead elected to rely solely on the guns and mortars to reduce the fort. However, these being of such light calibre, they were unlikely to do more than annoy the garrison and damage the fittings. On the 27th a new battery was opened much closer to the fort, but this was soon silenced and, as a last resort, heated shot was tried on the 29th. This, at last, had some effect but Scott responded with a sortie on the 31st that overran the Jacobite battery, capturing five pieces, spiking three more, and taking prisoner one of the

French artillerymen. By this stage, it was clear that Fort William could not be taken, and, with Cumberland again on the move, orders came for the French and Jacobite troops to return to Inverness. On the night of 2/3 April the siege, and most of the artillery, was abandoned.

While the original French contingent had been operating in the Western Highlands, more French troops had been arriving on the east coast. As noted in Chapter 1, the whole of the Régiment de Fitzjames was shipped out from Ostend, minus its horses, on board the privateers *Bourbon*, *Charité*, and *Prince de Nassau*. Only the latter, however, made it past the watchful Royal Navy to land 130 men at Aberdeen on 22 February: 396 officers and men on board the other two ships were taken prisoner.[14] Next sailed the Dunkirk component of the force; 650 men from the Régiments de Clare and Berwick under the command of the Marquis de Fimarçon. The convoy comprised five privateers acting as transports, and a fifth – the 16-gun *Comte de Maurepas* – acting as escort along with the 28-gun frigate *Emeraude*, a regular commissioned warship. This time, the blockade was evaded but when the convoy arrived off Aberdeen on 27 February they learned that the Jacobites had abandoned the port and withdrawn. Incredibly, rather than working northwards to make contact with the Jacobite army, the ships put about and returned to France, again safely dodging the patrolling British warships. The one exception was the privateer *l'Aventurier* which, having become detached, successfully landed the picquet of the Regiment de Berwick at Peterhead on the 25th. On the face of it, this demonstrates the foolishness of the main convoy having turned back; then again, though, the French ship was captured by the British 24-gun *Surprise* as she attempted to return to France, so whether the larger force could have successfully been landed is open to debate. Undoubtedly, though, the infusion of so large a contingent of fresh regular soldiers into the Jacobite army would have made a substantial difference to the course of the final campaign, although whether it would have been enough to alter the eventual outcome is rather more debatable.

It took some time to mount the French cavalry, a portion of whom received the cast-off horses from the Jacobite troopers of Lords Kilmarnock and Pitsligo while the remainder were compelled to do duty on foot. The infantrymen of Berwick, however, under *Capitaines* Nicholas de la Hoye and Patrick Clargue, were soon in action as part of a scheme concocted by the ever-active Nicholas Glascoe. Their objective was a Government outpost at Keith, from which Major General Humphrey Bland had recently evicted the Jacobite garrison as the Government army began to push forward to the line of the Spey. The outpost was manned by a company of the Argyll Militia and a detachment of 30 cavalrymen from Kingston's 10th Light Horse; Bland had left them there to tempt the Jacobites back, thinking that he could then catch them off guard, but Glascoe believed that they were ripe for the taking and came up with a scheme by which this could be achieved. For this he borrowed 16 men from the picquet of Berwick and 25 assorted cavalrymen

---

14  McLynn, *France and the Jacobite Rising*, p.192; other sources list 373 prisoners taken, and name the ship that successfully made it to Scotland as the *Sophie*.

(mostly Bagot's Hussars, with a few mounted volunteers) to add to a 200-man detachment from Ogilvie's Regiment.

Glascoe's detachment set out from Fochabers on the evening of 20 March, with the cavalry and the French infantry acting as vanguard. The direct march was eight miles but the attackers swung north around the town and then skirted it to the east so as to ultimately approach from the south. This, when they entered the town around midnight, allowed them to make the successful gambit of claiming to be reinforcements, something which was no doubt aided by the appearance of the Berwick detachment in their red *justaucorps* – assuming that there was light enough for the colour to be made out. Glascoe himself was with the party who disarmed the Government sentries by this ruse, although not before shots had been fired and the alarm raised. The various parties of Government troops put up a resistance for a time from the various buildings in which they were billeted, but were soon obliged to surrender around 70 prisoners were taken and hustled off to Inverness before a Government relief force could arrive. One man of the Régiment de Berwick was killed, apparently the only fatality in the Jacobite force, and five of the enemy including one sentry personally dispatched by Glascoe. As with so many of the small actions of the Rising, casualties were light but it was a smart bit of outpost work and a moral success for the Jacobites: in the latter respect, it was timely indeed, for news would soon come in of a disaster further north, in which men of the Régiment de Berwick was again engaged.

The belated dispatch of French reinforcements in the spring of 1746 was in response to pleas for aid by the Jacobites who were now running short of men and material to continue the campaign. Although by this stage the bulk of the Jacobite infantry was equipped with French or Spanish muskets, thanks to the supply shipments sent through the blockade, there was a lack of money to pay the men or secure supplies of food. A total of 500,000 livres had therefore been prepared and some of it had been shipped with the squadron commanded by the Marquis de Fimarçon. A small portion of this money had been landed from *l'Aventurier* at Peterhead, but the remainder returned to Dunkirk with the rest of the convoy. In order to get a portion of the specie to the Jacobites, a new expedition was prepared and a total of 252,000 livres embarked aboard the privateer *Prince Charles*, the former *Hazard* captured at Montrose. The idea was that this single fast ship, commanded by 27-year-old Irishman Richard Talbot, would be able to dodge the Royal Navy patrols and make it through to Scotland. A number of Franco-Irish officers accompanied the expedition officers – the total variously given as 14 and 22 – including Ignatious Browne, returning to Scotland after having carried the news of Falkirk to Versailles, and the whole was escorted by a picquet from the Régiment de Berwick.

It had been intended to land the shipment at Portsoy or Findhorn, on the coast between Inverness and Fraserburgh, but the fact that these harbours were still held by the Jacobites was known to the Royal Navy and a squadron was maintained to watch them. On the morning of 24 March, the *Prince Charles* was spotted and the British 20-gunner *Sheerness* – the same ship that had earlier captured the *Espérance* – was sent in pursuit. All through the day, and the following night, the two ships ran northwards in patchy and sometimes failing winds and then west as Talbot took his ship through the dangerous Pentland Firth. For a time he was able to break contact, but then, off the Kyle of Tongue, the *Sheerness* again hove into view. In desperation, Talbot tried to escape into the shallow waters of the Kyle itself – a long inlet formed where the River Kinloch ran into the sea – but instead grounded on the western coast of it. The *Sheerness* followed, guided by a local pilot, and dropped anchor opposite the grounded privateer a little before four in the afternoon on 25 March. Broadsides were exchanged but the *Prince Charles* was a sitting target – and outgunned to boot – and the French ship got by far the worst of it. Casualties mounted amongst the gunners, and by evening the survivors were being forced to keep their posts by the soldiers of the Régiment de Berwick.

The situation was clearly untenable, with masts and bowsprit shot away and water rising in the hold, but Talbot and Browne still hoped that by fighting on until nightfall they would at least be able to get the gold shipment away and thus carry out their mission even at the loss of their ship. During the night, the gold was got ashore and the ship abandoned, being taken possession of the next morning by a boarding party from the *Sheerness* who found a scene of carnage: 43 dead, and two men left on board too badly injured to be moved, from whom it was learned that a further 23 men were wounded but had made it ashore. Alas, the sacrifice was in vain for although the shore party made contact with a local Jacobite sympathiser he was obliged to tell them that the area was loyal to George II and could only offer his two sons as guides to help the party escape to the south. This they attempted to do, only to be intercepted by two companies of the local McKay clan militia backed up with regulars from Loudoun's 64th Highlanders. There was a brief, straggling fight in which the stranded party lost three men before surrendering but which bought time for much of the gold to be thrown into Loch Hacoin or into the heather, so that less than three-quarters of it was officially recovered (and, by all accounts, rather more of it privately gathered up). It was one thing, though, to try and deny the gold to the enemy but for it to end up anywhere other than in Jacobite coffers at Inverness was a major disaster. Furthermore, upon hearing of the loss of the gold Prince Charles sent the Earl of Cromartie with 1,500 men to try and recover it, depriving his army of more men whose presence would have been greatly beneficial with the main army now that the final showdown with Cumberland was looming.

## Culloden

The popular conception of the last battle of the '45 has little space for anything other than the heroic tragedy of the Jacobite charge against the Government infantry, which, although it proved to be the decisive point in the battle was by no means the only aspect of the fighting that day. The French contingent, united for the first time to put around 800 men on the field of battle, played an important role both in the battle and the events leading up to it, beginning with the screening operations on 12 April as the Government army pushed across the Spey to begin their final advance before the far-flung Jacobite army had completed its concentration.

At this stage, the troops from Fort William had not yet re-joined, nor had the men that Lord George Murray had taken into the Athol country. Thus, the Spey, which might otherwise have proved an effective line of defence although O'Sullivan thought it too extended a position due to the numerous fords, was covered by a skeleton force of only 2,000 men. This was under Lord John Drummond assisted by his ailing brother, and fellow lieutenant general, the Duke of Perth. His force included the picquet of the Régiment de Berwick and the mounted element of the Régiment de Fitzjames; the latter numbered approximately 70 troopers, under the command of *Capitaine* Robert Shea. The Government movement caught the Jacobites off their guard, so that Cumberland's advance guard of light horse, Highlanders, and grenadiers were able to cross the Ford of Bellie, a mile below Fochabers, with little opposition. Soon the Jacobite forces were soon tumbling back through Nairn in some disorder, their outlying units on the right of the line having had to hurry to extricate themselves lest they be cut off. O'Sullivan explained what happened next:

Sullivan… got a horse back, past the bridge of Nairn with the Duke of Perth, the houssards & some of the Guardes, to go & reconnoitre the enemy yt was in full march but not near enough to be seen from the Town. They went a quarter of a mil from the Town until they saw the enemy plainly upon several Colomns, then they came back, Sullivan prayd Ld Balmerino, who was there with his company of guards, & never mist an occasion, to go with Captn Shea yt commanded fitz James's Squadron, & set themselves on one ligne wth the houssards, along the river side, their left to the Town, make the greatest appearance they cou'd, & wait there until he'd send for them. The Duke & Sullivan waited on a hight near the bridge until the enemy was very near them, then the Duke & Ld John retired with the foot. Sullivan kept Berwick's picquet with him, compos'd of three officers and twenty five men; he got the sergent & some of those men to set two or three little Turf Carts on the bridge, & set fire to them. This done, the enemy just over against, Sullivan retired, joyn'd the horse & form'd them on the high road, about two musquet shots from the Town and marched. A moment after the enemy's horse appears in the plaine formed & in march again us. Sullivan forms his little Cavalry likewise, but made a poor figure over against nine squadrons, & sends to the Duke of Perth to pray him, to leave him five hundred of the foot. Sullivan continued his retraite, makeing volte face from time to time alternatively with the smal number of horse he had & those five & twenty men of Berwick's. Four Battallions of the enemy joyns their horse, they continue to pursue Sullivan, fireing from time to time but were not near enough to do any hurt. Sullivan sent again to the Duke of Perth to pray him to leave him a hundred & fifty men or even fifty but the Duke and Ld John, went to meet the prince yt was in march towards them with the rest of the Army, & not a soul wou'd wait for Sullivan. He continued his retreat so, for four mils, before he joyned the foot with nine squadrons and four battallions at his heels, haveing alwaise part of this little Cavalry faceing towards them, & hat in all yt time but a trooper & two horse of fitz James wounded. When the enemy saw yt he joyned the foot, they pursued no farther.[15]

---

15   O'Sullivan, *1745 and After*, pp.152-153.

Again, the steadiness of the French regulars had proven its value.

Having extricated itself from Nairn, and with most – but not all – of the outlying forces now on hand, the Jacobite army prepared itself for the battle that needed to be fought to cover its base of operations at Inverness. The days leading up to Culloden, however, were marked with moves and counter-moves as Charles and his staff officers sought to establish the best site for a showdown with Cumberland. Lord George Murray had begun the process on the 13th, sending two of his aides de camp, Henry Kerr of Graden and *Capitaine* Kennedy, *aide-major* of the Régiment de Bulkeley, to scout the ground between Inverness and Nairn. They selected a position near Dalcross Castle, covered by a ravine, but this was rejected by O'Sullivan as it restricted the army's ability to manoeuvre. Another site, reconnoitred two days later by Kerr and *Brigadier* Stapleton, was potentially even stronger but meant withdrawing south of the River Nairn and thus uncovering the road to Inverness. This, too, was rejected and O'Sullivan himself selected a position, on Drumossie Moor but a mile or so to the east of the actual battlefield. This position was occupied on 15 April but no attack materialised, leading to the adoption of Lord George Murray's proposal for a night attack on the Government camp at Nairn.

Although dismissed as a gamble, the concept of the night attack was a sound one that met the approval of the Jacobite high command: it was, indeed, one of the few operations about which O'Sullivan and Murray – who had been bickering more than ever during the previous days as Murray sought repeatedly to tinker with the army's dispositions and order of battle – were in agreement. However, once the march was underway matters soon descended into confusion and farce, as the column became strung out and delayed in the dark and the rain. The French regular infantry, deployed in the rear with the Prince, was not at its best on an operation of this sort and could not keep pace with the Highlanders, but even the Highlanders could not make it into position in time. Realising this, Murray, with the vanguard, turned his men about but in the confusion it took time for the word to get around and the result was that the army straggled back onto Drumossie Moor wet, tired, and hungry. *Capitaine* Shee was sent with his half-squadron of the Régiment de Fitzjames to bring up supplies from Inverness, but was still in the town when word was received that the Government army was advancing from Nairn and that battle was imminent. It was all that the French troopers could do to saddle up and return to the Moor themselves in time to join the fight.

The numbers of Jacobites present on the field at Culloden is impossible to pinpoint exactly, but a figure in the region of 6,000 is a realistic top estimate. Indeed, the actual total may very well be lower than that if one makes allowance for men who had not re-joined after the night march, or who had gone off in search of food and: a figure as low as 5,000 has been suggested as a more realistic total. Around 800 of these men were in the ranks of the French regular units, which works out as something in the region of one man in seven and represents the largest French contribution to any battle of the '45. Breaking down the French numbers is, however, a little problematic, with conflicting sources and interpretations that need some picking through.

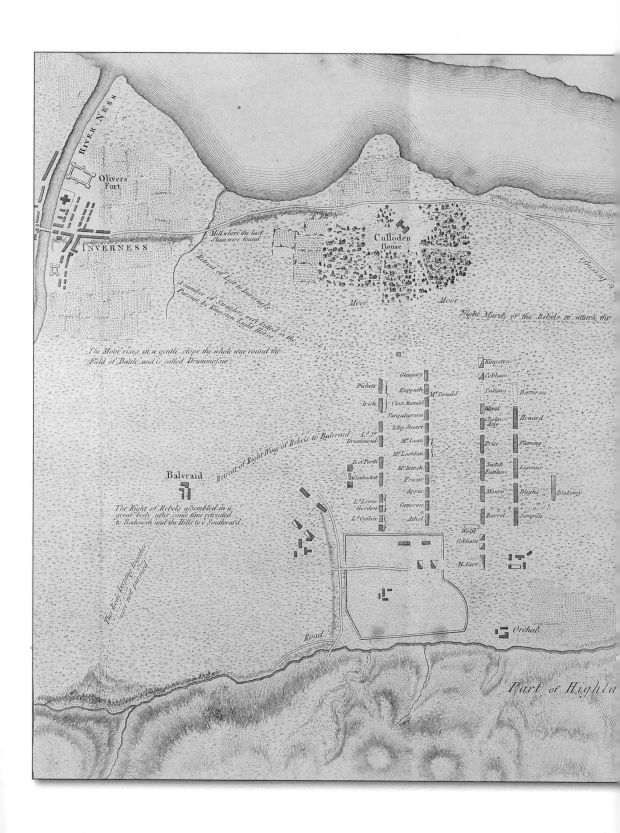

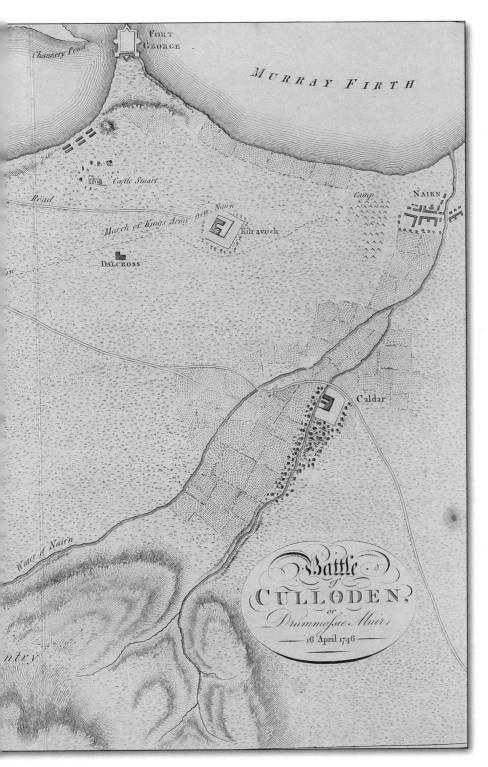

Map of the Culloden battlefield and environs from John Home's 1802 *The History of the Rebellion in the Year 1745*. Although it contains a few inaccuracies – notably representing the Irish Picquets as two battalions and omitting the walls that surrounded the Culloden Park – the broad coverage of this map helps contextualise the scope of the area over which the armies marched and fought in the lead up to the battle and on the day itself.

The Royal Ecossois, to begin with, represents the easiest unit to total, since the men in the ranks all came from one unit, fought together as a unit, and are enumerated by the Marquis d'Eguilles as having been 350-strong just before the battle. Allowing for wastage on campaign, partially counteracted by local recruiting, this seems a reasonable figure based on the assumed strength after landing of 400 men. The squadron of the Régiment de Fitzjames is also relatively easy to account for as it had seen no appreciable action before Culloden and can therefore be assumed to have mustered the full 131 men that Eguilles credited it with; the issue that is harder to account for is how many of them were mounted; most modern histories agree on a total of around 70, with the remainder forming a dismounted detachment attached to the Irish Picquets.

The composition of the Irish Picquets at Culloden is the most awkward to calculate. Eguilles reckoned that the original battalion had been reduced by half, but that having incorporated an impressive total of 148 prisoners, deserters, and other miscellaneous extras the unit actually totalled 260 men. This suggests 112 survivors from the original three picquets, which would actually suggest that they had lost more like a third of their starting strength of around 170. If they really had lost half of their starting strength, one can only get to the 112 figure if the picquet of the Régiment de Berwick is also included but Eguilles enumerated this separately with a strength of 42 men. O'Sullivan, in the account quoted above, refers to having three officers and 25 men of the Régiment de Berwick with him at Nairn, and from this it has been inferred that this was the total strength of the picquet. However, O'Sullivan does not explicitly say that this was the case and it seems unlikely that so many men had been lost since landing, particularly since we know of only the one fatality in the fight at Keith. Thus, Eguilles' figure of 42 seems sensible and by that count there were 302 men in the ranks of the Irish Picquets at Culloden, to which must be added any dismounted troopers of the Régiment de Fitzjames. There is not, it must be said, any concrete evidence that this is where these men were placed, but since they do not appear as an independent unit in any account of the action it is hard to see where else they would have ended up and, as we have seen, the men had all been issued with infantry muskets for dismounted duty so would have been perfectly capable of performing in this role. The only alternative interpretation is that they had gone back to Inverness as part of Shea's mission to obtain supplies, and did not take part in the battle at all. However, if the dismounted troopers were present then this suggests a unit total of around 360 for the Irish Picquets as a battalion. Lastly, there were also an unspecified number of French artillerymen on the field and they were joined by at least one officer of engineers during the course of the battle.

The deployment of the Jacobite army at Culloden on 16 April 1746 represents a disposition that was as close as was ever achieved to its theoretical ideal battle structure of Highland regiments in the first line, Lowland units in the second, and the cavalry and French regulars forming a reserve. Rather than being formed as a single body, however, the French infantry was divided with the Royal Ecossois and Irish Picquets each forming a single full-strength battalion rather than a combined composite unit as at Falkirk. The fact that the French infantry was at full strength also meant that it was possible to assign to them a role which had been envisaged for them at Falkirk but which had not materialised due to their late arrival and small numbers at that battle, namely to form an anchor for each flank of the Jacobite army to prevent the flanks being turned. This deployment seems to have been a brainchild of Lord George Murray's as it was he who had the greatest influence over the army's dispositions on the field; it was certainly Murray who had proposed this distribution of things at Falkirk, so revisiting the idea three months later seems fitting. Murray appears to have envisaged the Irish Picquets covering the right flank, which was anchored on the Culwhiniac enclosure, and the Royal Ecossois the left flank, anchored on the walled parks of Culloden House, but in fact the actual deployment was the reverse of this.

The squadron of the Regiment de Fitzjames was deployed on the right of the third line along with Lord Elcho's Troop of Lifeguards. Some accounts credit *Capitaine* Shea and 16 men as forming part of the escort for Prince Charles, but this seems to be a conflation of the fact that, on the one hand, the Prince did have an escort of 16 men from Lord Balmerino's Troop of Lifeguards, and, on the other, that Shea near the end of the battle was tasked with getting the Prince safely off the field as we shall see. It does not follow that Shea spent the whole battle guarding the Prince, and to have broken up the Jacobite army's only effective battlefield cavalry unit when the prince already had a mounted bodyguard unit seems a foolish dispersal that would have diluted the effectiveness of the French squadron to little purpose.

Tucked away as they were, the French troops were spared the attentions of the opening bombardment, which commenced around one o'clock in the afternoon, and remained as spectators as the Jacobite front line shuffled up to its left in preparation for the charge. They would have watched, too, as Lowland regiments from the second line were fed forwards to fill up the gaps in the first, and as O'Sullivan discretely shifted two of Lord Lewis Gordon's battalions to the left in order to be in position to counter any move through the Culwhiniac enclosure. Murray had previously blocked such a move, but O'Sullivan's initiative was all to the good, for Lieutenant General Hawley and Major General Bland were already pushing into the enclosure with five squadrons of dragoons and a battalion of Government Highlanders. The combined result of these Jacobite redeployments was to significantly reduce the number of units available in reserve: essentially all that remained uncommitted were the two French battalions, the cavalry, Lord Kilmarnock's Foot Guards (a grand name for a composite battalion of understrength infantry units and dismounted cavalrymen), and the two battalions of Ogilvie's Regiment.

After 20 or so minutes' firing, the Jacobite front line began to move forwards, concentrating its charge against the left of Cumberland's infantry. Unlike at Prestonpans and Falkirk, the Government infantry stood its ground, and the result was carnage. Within minutes, those Highlanders on the Jacobite right who had survived the charge were falling back whilst the Jacobite left, hampered by boggy ground, never charged home as a body at all but instead attacked piecemeal and failed to achieve anything like the impact of those acting on the dryer ground. The battle was clearly lost, but it was by

The ground initially occupied by the Irish Picquets at Culloden, viewed looking back from the main Jacobite position. (Photo by Raymond Finlayson)

no means over and there was hard fighting ahead in which the French units would play an important role.

As the Highlanders made their charge, the two French battalions both moved up to provide supporting fire; it is not clear whether the Irish Picquets were actively engaged at this point, but the Royal Ecossois exchanged volleys with Campbell's 21st Fusiliers in the centre of the Government first line. This was probably the best employment for the regular infantry, who could not have kept up with the Highlanders in their charge. The only other possible role that seems viable during the offensive stage of the battle would have been to push the French troops into the Culwhiniac enclosure to cover the flank of the main attack but such a movement would have set up a head-on collision with the advancing Government dragoons and it is hard to envisage what the end result of such a meeting might have been. All in all, it was probably as well that the regulars were held in reserve, where they were at least able to help extricate the surviving Jacobite Highlanders streaming back from the failed charge.

By this point in the battle, the Government dragoons had passed through the Culwhiniac enclosure and were facing off against Lord Lewis Gordon's battalions in the Jacobite right-rear. The Government Highlanders, however, remained in the enclosure and fired upon the Jacobites as they fell back before beginning to advance over the wall. They were met by the Royal Ecossois, which had wheeled to the right after breaking off its exchange of fire with Campbell's 21st and now advanced to meet them. After an initial clash in which Captain John Campbell of Ballimore, commanding the Government battalion, was killed, both parties fell back. The Royal Ecossois were now pulled into an ad hoc line of infantry running from the walls of the enclosure down to where the battalions of Lord Lewis Gordon's were endeavouring to check the advance of the Government dragoons, in which role they had now been joined by the two battalions of Ogilvie's Regiment. These four Lowland battalions between them occupied the attentions of Kerr's 11th Dragoons, but two squadrons of Cobham's 10th were able to pass between the Lowland infantry and the Culwhiniac enclosure and thus cut off such Jacobite troops who were still fighting along the line of its northern wall. The mainstay of this force, Kilmarnock's Foot Guards having decamped, was the Royal Ecossois and they were now in serious trouble.

Exactly what befell the battalion at this point is not entirely clear. There was evidently some hard fighting here, in which, amongst other casualties, *Lieutenant-Colonel* Lord Louis Drummond of Melfort was badly wounded, losing a leg. In all, the battalion lost some 50 or so men in the course of the battle but certainly some of these would have been sustained in the earlier fighting and so it is not necessary to postulate a bloodbath or last stand at this juncture. What is certain is that the battalion was broken, and a portion of it cut off and forced to surrender – eight officers and perhaps 40 or so rank and file.[16] The remainder of the battalion managed to cut its way out with its colours and join the surviving units of the Jacobite right wing in escaping across the River Nairn to the south of the battlefield. The survivors of the Royal Ecossois eventually made it to the post-battle rendezvous at Ruthven Barracks under the command of *Capitaine* Matthew Hale, the *aide-major*. The historian Stuart Reid speculates that they were able to withdraw by wings, or half-battalions, which would seem a logical explanation of how one portion got off in good order but at least a part of the other wing was badly cut up.[17]

On the other flank, meanwhile, the Irish element of the French contingent was also fighting hard. Having seen the failure of the Highlanders' charge and recognising that the day was lost, O'Sullivan reported that he ran 'to Shea yt Commanded fitz James's Squadron & tels him "Yu see all is going to pot. Yu can be of no great succor, so before a general deroute wch will soon be, Seize upon the Prince and take him off"'. Note that there is no mention of Shea having had responsibility for the Prince prior to this point. O'Sullivan was aware that an enemy mounted regiment was moving up on the right of the Government line and posed both a serious threat to the troops on this

---

16  The latter figure is calculated on the fact that, per Reid, *1745*, p.213, 222 rank and file prisoners were taken on the field from French units but that c.160 of these would have been from the Irish Picquets – which lost around half their strength – and a portion of the remainder from the cavalry and artillery.

17  See Reid's chapter 'The Battle of Culloden: A Narrative Account' in Tony Pollard (ed.), *Culloden. The History and Archaeology of the Last Clan Battle* (Barnsley: Pen and Sword 2009), p.126.

Monument to the stand by the Royal Ecossois and the Lowland battalions of Ogilvie and Lord Lewis Gordon.
(Photo by Raymond Finlayson)

part of the field and to the Prince's person. He therefore instructed Shea that if he was pursued he could turn his squadron to face them and 'at least he cou'd by standing ferm a little give him [i.e. the Prince] time to escape'.[18] Thus did the mounted element of the French contingent leave the field of battle.

The horsemen that had excited O'Sullivan's concerns were in fact a mixed body of three squadrons – two from Kingston's 10th Light Horse and one from Cobham's 10th Dragoons – which had formed the mounted element on the Government right wing. They had circled round the extremity of the Jacobite left, and were poised to take the Clan Macdonald regiments in the flank as they fell back. To forestall this, O'Sullivan ordered the Irish Picquets to drive them off, and, in his own terse relation of what happened, 'Stapleton makes an evolution or two, fires at the Dragoons and oblidges them to retire', whereupon the Macdonalds took advantage of the respite to join the withdrawal to Inverness.[19] The Picquets, meanwhile, threw themselves into the Culloden Park enclosures which were already occupied by an ad hoc gun detachment of French artillerymen commanded by the contingent's junior officer of engineers, *Capitaine* Charles du Saussay, who had brought up a 4-pounder from Inverness during the morning and deployed it as the battle was underway.

This all makes it sound very orderly and calm, but Stuart Reid has hypothesised, based on relative casualty figures, that matters went far less smoothly and that the Picquets paid dearly for having drawn down the attention of the Government horsemen. Reid suggests that the horsemen got in amongst the withdrawing infantry and that it was at this point that heavy casualties began to be inflicted upon the Picquets.[20] This is possible, certainly, but it seems unlikely that a battalion so badly broken as Reid suggests could have rallied so soon and put up so desperate a resistance thereafter as the Picquets undoubtedly did; conversely, if the battalion was not broken, it is inconceivable that their opponents would have suffered so few losses against them if it came to close-quarters fighting. What seems most likely is that the initial volley from the Picquets emptied a few saddles and made the horsemen rein in their advance, and that thereafter Stapleton had his men fall back – perhaps by wings, as Reid hypothesises the Royal Ecossois attempted to do, but with more success – until they had reached the shelter of the walls and linked up with du Saussay and his gunners.

With the high stone walls as a breastwork, and du Saussay's men firing their 4-pounder through a breach that they had made, the position occupied by the Picquets was a strong one as the walls covered them from the attentions of the cavalry. What was more, the proximity of the Culloden Park to the Inverness road also meant that a pursuit along that axis by the Government right wing was problematic until the French had been winkled out. This therefore became a priority operation, which drew in a considerable portion of the Government right wing. The position was eventually suppressed by fire

---

18  O'Sullivan, *1745 and After*, pp.164-165.
19  O'Sullivan, *1745 and After*, p.165.
20  Stuart Reid, *Like Hungry Wolves. Culloden Moor 16 April 1746* (London: Windrow and Green, 1994), p.109.

from coehorn mortars, which could lob their bombs over the walls, and four 3-pounder cannon. While the guns were being brought up the Picquets were also engaged by the infantry of the Government right wing, and a musket ball from one of these soldiers hit Stapleton just below the heart, inflicting a mortal wound. *Capitaine* Stack, commanding the Picquet of Lally, was also wounded but unlike his commander he survived the battle.

At length, du Saussay's lone gun was overwhelmed by the fire of the Government artillery and the position had to be abandoned. Whilst it is an indisputable fact that the Irish Picquets lost half their strength that day, it seems to this author most likely that the bulk of them fell at this point, under the fire of the combined Government artillery and musketry, but there were sufficient men still on their feet to attempt to make it to Inverness. This they came close to doing – or, at least, a portion of them did for there were 50 or so French prisoners picked up along the road during the course of the afternoon – but at length they surrendered on the advice of the Marquis d'Eguilles and thus brought the day's action to an end.

Of the remaining French troops who had escaped to the south-west, the majority turned themselves in over the coming days once it became clear that the Rising was well and truly over and that Prince Charles had left them. The remnants of the Royal Ecossois came back to Inverness to surrender on 19 April along with those men of the Régiment de Fitzjames who had helped see the Prince off the field. Some individuals – particularly those who felt that they were at risk through nationality or prior service in the British Army – melted away, or at least tried to, whilst those who were confident of the protection afforded by their status as French soldiers gave themselves up. Sir John Macdonald, for example, decided that he was too old for a life on the run in the mountains and so betook himself to Inverness with the Royal Ecossois; Matthew Hale on the other hand, preferred to take his chances on the run than as an Englishman in a French uniform, and joined a party of fugitives that also included Lord John Drummond and the Duke of Perth. The engineer Mirabelle was picked up by a detachment of the Argyll Militia near Balquihidder on 1 May; after first heading for Fort Augustus on a rumour that the Prince was rallying forces there he had then attempted to double back to Montrose to find a ship but had been headed off by Government patrols. O'Sullivan accompanied the Prince on his own escape. With its officers and men thus surrendered or dispersed, the role of the French contingent in the '45 was at an end.

5

# After the Rising

## Tribulations and Trials

Even as plans were being made for the last-ditch attempts to get men and funding from France to Scotland, the Jacobite ship-owners Walsh and O'Heguerty had begun to make plans for the rescue of Prince Charles in the event that the Rising collapsed. They initially proposed to buy and refit the battered *Elisabeth* for a mission to Scotland, but Walsh eventually persuaded Maurepas to fund an expedition from Nantes by the privateers *Mars* and *Bellone*. With a cargo of arms they were to cruise off the west coast of Scotland, with a view either to aiding the Prince if the Jacobite cause was able to rally in the Western Highlands or effecting a rescue if all collapsed and it was necessary to bring Charles back to France. Jacobites in France pursued similar ideas in the aftermath of Culloden, with grandiose proposals for the dispatch of multiple battalions from ports in Brittany to revive the Rising and undo the disaster inflicted on Drumossie Moor. Other proposals called for the Brest Fleet to be diverted from Maurepas' scheme to recapture Louisbourg and embark troops for a descent on Ireland.

Maurepas, surprisingly, seems to have given these schemes some consideration but ultimately did not deviate from his preoccupation with affairs across the Atlantic. Accordingly, it was Walsh's expedition that proved to be the main effort insofar as post-Culloden operations were concerned. The *Mars* and *Bellone* arrived off Scotland at the end of April 1746 and put into Loch nan Uamh in Moidart, the same location at which the Prince had disembarked from *La Doutelle* 10 months previously. A number of fugitives reached the rendezvous, including Jacobite nobleman Lord Elcho and also the party led by Lord John Drummond. Measures were set in train to land the arms and money that had been brought across, but these were disrupted by the arrival of a British flotilla comprising the 20-gun *Greyhound*, 14-gun *Baltimore*, and bomb vessel *Terror*. The French ships were both small frigates, so had a comfortable advantage in gun-power but were restricted by the shallow and enclosed waters. After a six-hour action on 2 May the British warships were driven off but it was a hard fight and one of the casualties was *Capitaine* Matthew Hale, *aide-major* of the Royal Ecossois, who refused to take cover below decks and paid for his gallantry with his life. The remaining fugitives were safely embarked for France, although the ailing Duke of Perth died at sea before the ships reached their destination.

This expedition was all well and good, of course, and the gold that had been offloaded would fund more escapes in the future, but the main preoccupation in France – and the more so in Rome, where James III was furious that Drummond and his party had left Scotland without their Prince – was the rescue of Charles. This was eventually completed on 20 September when the Prince was embarked with a number of companions including the wounded clan chief Donald Cameron of Locheil aboard a pair of privateers – *Le Conti* and *l'Heureux* – that had sailed from Saint Malo as part of an expedition organised by Richard Warren. Safe from the attentions of the Royal Navy, the Prince was put ashore at Roscoff on 11 October (NS). O'Sullivan, who had separated from Charles during their wanderings in the Highlands and Islands, had previously been picked up from Benbecula in July in yet another privateer, *Le Hardi Mendiant*; he would re-join the French service as a staff officer, and be awarded a baronetcy in the Jacobite peerage, but he disappears from the historical record after the war's end. Other leading Jacobites including Lord Ogilvie had made their escapes via Norway.

After the safety of the Prince, the other main French preoccupation was the fate of the officers and men who had fallen into British hands during the events of the Rising. These amounted to 84 officers and 728 other ranks, the greater part of them coming from the men captured at sea from the Régiment de Fitzjames and the Picquets of Bulkeley, Clare, and Berwick. Negotiations had begun in January 1746 for the exchange of those men already in captivity, even before the defeat at Culloden served to further increase their numbers, but matters quickly stalled due to France having failed to honour the terms of a previous prisoner exchange. It took the draconian enforcement of the policy of arresting anyone of British origin who was in France without a passport – which previously seems only to have been used as a means of scooping up likely recruits – to bring matters to a head but, even so, it would be 1747 before the last of the prisoners were exchanged.

Not all of the men taken captive were treated in the same way, however. Regular French officers were treated as ordinary prisoners but, as we have seen, the officers commissioned into the Royal Ecossois during the Rising were treated differently and suffered far harsher penalties. A special case was also made for Charles Radclyffe, 5th Earl of Derwentwater, who was amongst the officers captured aboard the *Esperance*. He had been condemned to death for treason for his part in the '15, for which his brother, the 3rd Earl, was executed, but had escaped from gaol and made his way to France. Although he had obtained a captaincy in the Régiment de Dillon, this did not save him and he was executed on 8 December 1746 under the terms of his original sentence, the imposition of which preceded his having entered French service.

A number of other officers who were not of French birth also had some legal difficulty, being put on trial for treason. *Capitaine* James Hay, for example, paymaster of the Royal Ecossois, was found guilty and condemned at Carlisle but was included on a list of those to be considered for clemency:

This man petitions for Mercy, & says that he has been a long time in the French service.

The French officers presented a protest to Mr Webb about this man in very high terms, & behaved with great Indecency to the Chief Baron Parker upon Hay's being convicted.[1]

Hay's sentence of death was in due course changed to one of banishment, which was the fate of most of the French officers who went through this process. Only Derwentwater, on the strength of his pre-existing conviction, and Duncan Colquohoun as a deserter from the British Army, went to the scaffold.

The response of the captive French officers to these trials, as outlined in the case of Hay, was understandable for they all relied on their commissions to ensure their eventual safe release and exchange. A similar plea was made on behalf of Guillaume Moore of the Royal Ecossois:

*Capitaine* Charles Radclyffe, 5th Earl of Derwentwater. (Public Domain)

Mr Moore Ensign in Drummond's Regiment in the King of France's Service aged eighteen years, has been three years in the French Service, Went to Scotland by orders with his corps. Which he never left but Surrendered with the rest after the Battle of Culloden. Notwithstanding the other officers of the Corps were made prisoners at large upon their Parole he was sent up to London, in the spring as a State Prisoner and he has Ever Since been Confined in Irons in the New Gaol Southwark it has been promised he shou'd be moved into the Marshalsea as a French Prisoner of War but as yet with no Effect.[2]

Moore was eventually pardoned on condition of banishment, and returned to France where he later rose to the rank of *capitaine*. It is not clear why he was singled out for this treatment, although a possible answer might be his having been listed as being of Irish birth in the intelligence report on the officers of the Royal Ecossois put together in September 1745 from the reports of deserters.

Another officer who found himself in a difficult position was Nicolas Glascoe, who was taken prisoner whilst wearing the civilian clothes that he had adopted whilst serving with Lord Ogilvie's Regiment. He was therefore obliged to demonstrate that he was indeed, as he claimed, a French-born *lieutenant* in the Régiment de Dillon and therefore due the treatment appropriate for his rank and nationality. Glascoe had surrendered himself

---

1 'List of the Prisoners condemned at Carlisle Who have petitioned for Mercy, or have been recommended as Objects thereof, by the Judges, Jury, Mr Webb, or other Persons', TNA, SP36/91, Part I, p.9.

2 Undated and anonymous appeal, TNA, SP36/91, Part I, p.40.

THE LILIES AND THE THISTLE

near Ruthven on 19 April 1746, and clearly had no expectation that he would be singled out: had he had such fears, he would have presumably remained with Lord Ogilvie and the other senior officers of Ogilvie's Regiment in their flight to Norway. As he outlined in a petition to the Duke of Cumberland, he had been for 20 years, 'and even from his infancy', in the service of King Louis and requested that he be considered for exchange 'and in the meantime to be treated as a Prisoner of War and as a Military Officer of his Most Christian Majesty, and not be held in His Britannic Majesty's Civil Courts of Justice'.[3]

Notwithstanding this appeal, sufficient witnesses were found to prove that Glascoe had served as a major in Ogilvie's Regiment, and he was accordingly brought to trial on 10 November 1746. The resulting verdict was reported to the Duke of Newcastle:

> This morning came on the Tryal of Mr Glascoe. We fully Proved by a Number of Witnesses his wearing the Highland dress and acting as Major to Lord Ogilvie's Second Battalion. That he Reviewed and Exercised them as such, and constantly marched and acted with them in that Capacity and was always reputed major in that Corps. And we proved by Capn. Eyre that when he Examined him by His Royal Highness the Duke's Order he said he was a Lieutenant in Dillon's Regiment but Owned he was an Irishman born at Dublin. Mr Jodrell his Council rested his defence, 1st on his being a native of France, 2dly upon the foot of the Cartell of Frankfort. He called Six Witnesses to prove his being a native of France who Spoke to his having been in the French Service and in Dillon's Regiment since 1725 when he was not above 10 years Old. That he then spoke very broken English but very good French. That his Christopher Glascoe his Father was a Captain in that Regiment and was generally reputed to have left Ireland under the Treaty of Limerick. That this Christopher and the Prisoner Conversed as Father & Son. And that his ffather [sic] frequently Declared the prisoner was born at St. Germains en Laye. That he was reputed by all in the Regiment to be born at St. Germains en Laye. That all those concur in that Regiment tho' born in France, yet if born of Irish parents, always called themselves, and were called by officers, Irish. That his Mother's name was a ffrench [sic] one. That he was Ordered by Lord John Drummond contrary to his own Inclination to Serve with Lord Ogilvie's Regiment to instruct them in their Exercise under pain of being broke and sent to France. That Several of the French Officers wore Highland Dress to prevent their being Mistaken in the night by the Highlanders for the English – two of the their Private Men having been shot by the Highlanders under that Mistake. He likewise produced a Certificate of his Birth which agreed with the Account his Witnesses gave and had the Appearance of a Genuine Real Certificate, but not being able to give that proof the law required it could not be read. The Prisoner Owned he Declared to Captain Eyre he was Born at Dublin but Declared his reason was that being informed Capn. Eyre was a Native of Ireland he thought he would be more favourable to his Countryman. This Evidence being Satisfactory to the Court as to his being a French Man and indeed to all of us we did not call another Witness we had and whom we intended to produce in reply who was Mr Glascoe's servant

---

3    Petition, Glascoe to Cumberland, TNA, SP36/91, Part I, p.56.

in Scotland, and to whom he had Declared he was a native of Ireland, and that he left Ireland and went to France when he was about 13 Years Old. Neither was the Point of the Cartell gone into, but the Attorney General Submitted without going any further to the Jury's finding him Not Guilty which they accordingly did.[4]

Having been freed by the civil court, Glascoe was promptly re-detained as a prisoner of war and eventually exchanged with the other French officers.

The treatment of the rank and file prisoners followed much the same pattern as did that of the officers. Those who were known to have deserted from the British service were for the most part extracted from the rest, tried for their crime, and sentenced accordingly – which meant transportation in most cases and execution for those of whom it was felt necessary to make an example. Some thought was evidently given to special treatment for those men who had enlisted since the outbreak of war, even if they had not served the British crown prior to entering French service. In Captain Eyre's report, those men from the batch of Fitzjames prisoners investigated at Canterbury who had enlisted since the war had begun were singled out, their details being listed again at the end of the main return, with the annotation that 'General Dalzell wou'd willingly have these men, to recruit His Regiment in the Leward [*sic*] Islands'.[5] A similar annotation was made at the end of Eyre's report of the prisoners at Berwick-upon-Tweed, but it does not seem that any French prisoners were sent to the fever islands, presumably for fear of retribution against British prisoners in French hands. Dalzell's 38th Foot had been in the West Indies since 1707, hence its manpower problems, but had to make do with 250 Jacobite prisoners to fill up its ranks.

Conversely, those who had deserted *from* the French service whilst in Scotland – such as the brothers Joseph and William Boes, who had absconded from the Picquet of Rooth during the operations against Forts Augustus and William and are identified by Stuart Reid as having robbed the fugitive Lifeguard John Daniel – were given their discharge and allowed to go free.[6] Other prisoners secured their own liberty, or attempted to do so, as reported in the *London Evening Post* of 6 May 1746:

> Last Monday Night four Soldiers endeavour'd to get out of Maidstone Gaol; they got upon the Leads for that Purpose, and having tied a Cord round a small Chimney, one of them letting him-self down, pull'd the Chimney after him, upon which the Guard was alarm'd, and the other three secur'd. He that got off was nam'd John Rossal, belonging to Fitz-James's Regiment of Horse in the French Service, was a Man of a black Complexion, had short Hair, about five Feet ten Inches high, with a light Drab Coat, and a Buff-colour'd Waistcoat.

---

4   Sharpe to Newcastle, 10 November 1746, TNA, SP36/89, Part I, p.77. The Cartel of Frankford, concluded 18 July 1744, was the Anglo-French agreement respecting the treatment of prisoners of war, by which all prisoners were to be either exchanged or ransomed with 15 days.

5   'A Return of the Prisoners of Fitzjames's Regiment of Horse, now Confin'd at Canterbury', TNA, SP36/89, pp.5-6.

6   On the Boes brothers see *Muster Roll*, p.137; Reid, *1745*, pp.174, 181, although Reid credits Joseph as having belonged to the Royal Ecossois.

It will be remembered that in Captain Eyre's list of the prisoners at Canterbury, another *maître*, one James Gaffney, had escaped from that gaol. Aside from those like Rossal and Gaffney who made their own arrangements, the remaining rank and file prisoners were eventually repatriated along with their officers.

## The Reckoning

The successful extrication of Prince Charles Edward Stuart from Scotland marked the end of active French involvement with the Jacobites. Although France had expended considerable amounts of treasure on their behalf, the Stuarts and their supporters had provided a useful distraction that gave France the necessary window of opportunity to revive her war effort and refocus her strategic goals. In the Low Countries, Saxe continued his successful campaign. Cumberland, who had returned to the Continent to resume command of the allied armies, was defeated again at Lauffeld on 2 July (NS) 1747 and the French went on to capture the fortress of Bergen-op-Zoom which fell in September of that year after a nine-week siege and was brutally sacked. The reconstituted Royal Ecossois took part on the French side, facing the similarly-reconstituted Loudoun's 64th Highlanders who were part of the garrison. Even at Lauffeld, the British contingent of Cumberland's army had not yet been restored to the numbers fielded for the Fontenoy campaign, underlining the importance of the '45 Rising in distracting the British from their Continental commitments. Saxe's string of conquests would ensure that France was able to go to the negotiating table in 1748 with a whole basket of bargaining chips with which to barter for the return of her lost colonies. This was all to the well, since Maurepas' vaunted expedition to recover Louisbourg had ended in disaster, with the Brest Fleet under *Lieutenant Général* the Duc d'Anville crippled by disease and dispersed by storms. The French fortress was, however, returned under the terms of the Treaty of Aix-la-Chapelle, which finally brought the war to an end.

It is hard to escape the conclusion that French support for the Jacobites was cynical and limited. For all of the genuine enthusiasm for the Stuart cause emanating from Tencin and even from Louis XV, any chance of a consistent and workable plan to support the Rising was scuppered by ministers who were all too busy with their own pet schemes. Maurepas soon fell from favour, though, another victim of the intrigues of La Pompadour, and the brothers d'Argenson likewise fell from grace; the Marquis in 1747 when it was clear that his foreign policy had failed in all respects, and the Comte a decade later due to his disapproval of the new alliance with the old enemy Austria. The Stuart Princes, too, were soon gone from the French court, banished as one of the terms of the Treaty of Aix-la-Chapelle: briefly invited back in 1759 when France was again planning an invasion of the British Isles, Charles failed to impress a new generation of ministers who dismissed the prospect of Jacobite assistance in their schemes.

Had there been a single directing figure behind French policy in 1745, though, and had that figure been steadfast in supporting the Stuarts, it is difficult to envisage what more could have been achieved. After the invasion scheme of 1744 collapsed, it is hard to see how a major French-backed Rising was viable in the face of British control of the Narrow Seas. Charles' decision to go it alone in Scotland created a window of opportunity, and better coordination could perhaps have ensured that more French troops were available in Scotland, and at an earlier date, than was the case. A Jacobite invasion of England from Scotland in spring 1746, with all the forces at Charles' disposal and backed by the Irish Brigade at full strength, might have been enough to show the English Jacobites that Charles had the French support that they demanded if they were to rise. Equally, delaying operations would have cost the Jacobites valuable momentum and it is equally possible that this hypothetical Franco-Scots army might instead have found itself facing a counter-invasion of Scotland by Cumberland, Wade, or both thanks to the Government army having used the winter to complete its own preparations. In a less extravagant counterfactual, had the gold aboard the *Prince Charles* and the reinforcements brought by the Marquis de Fimarçon both made it ashore in Scotland in March 1746 then it is possible that the Jacobite cause could have been maintained longer in the field. Culloden, if fought at all, might have been a very different battle with a rejuvenated and reinforced Jacobite army and a prolonged campaign might have allowed the

Royal Ecossois officer c.1757 by Charles Lyall. This image depicts some of the changes made to the regiment's uniform post-1746, notably the adoption of white breeches rather than red. (Anne S.K. Brown Military Collection)

dispatch of more Irish Brigade reinforcements. The end result, one feels, would not have been in doubt though, and by throwing in more men and money at so late a stage France would only have prolonged the agonies inflicted on Scotland.

Ironically, the failure of the Rising was in some respects a boon to the French army since it provided a new wave of Jacobite exiles seeking military service. The Royal Ecossois was swiftly reconstituted, fighting, as we have seen, in the campaign of 1747 in the course of which Lord John Drummond, who had succeeded his childless brother as titular Duke of Perth, was killed in action at Bergen-op-Zoom. He was succeeded in the colonelcy of the regiment by Lord Louis Drummond, and Lord Louis was in turn succeeded as *Lieutenant-Colonel* by Lachlan Cuthbert. Later, during the Seven Years War, the colonelcy passed to Lord Elcho.

In addition to this, however, two new Scottish regiments were raised. One of these, the Régiment d'Albany, was short lived. It was created in late 1747, nominally for Prince Charles but with the actual colonelcy going to Cameron of Locheil. Locheil had been promised compensation by Charles in the event that the Rising failed, and the financial perks of a colonelcy were an ample provision for a life in exile. The *lieutenant-*

*colonel* was Cluny Macpherson, who was in fact in hiding in Scotland for the regiment's entire existence although he later tried to claim the back-pay that was due to him for his non-service in the role. The other officers were all Scots exiles, many of them from the clan regiment that Locheil had led in the Rising. Nearly all the men, however, were French or German, with only a smattering of Scots and a few English and Irish. The uniform of this regiment is not officially listed, although it seems to have consisted of a red *justaucorps* with white facings and white smallclothes; the colour of the buttons and hat lacing is unknown. A portrait of an officer with a blue coat faced in red and laced in silver, once thought to be of Locheil as *Mestre-de-Camp Propriétaire* of Albany, is now understood to be of his son as a *capitaine* in the Royal Ecossois and to depict the uniform of that regiment. Upon Locheil's death in October 1748, the regiment was disbanded.

Part of the reason that there were so few Scotsmen to fill the ranks of the Regiment d'Albany was that those who had not been enlisted for the Royal Ecossois had been snapped up by the other new Scottish unit, activated in February 1747, the Régiment d'Ogilvie. This was very notionally a continuation of the Jacobite Ogilvie's Regiment, which, as discussed, may or may not have been taken into French pay during the '45. Lord Ogilvie was granted the colonelcy and his *lieutenant-colonel* was Sir William Gordon of Park who had held that rank during the Rising as an officer of Pitsligo's Horse. The *major*, fittingly, was Nicolas Glascoe. All of the other officers were Scots, apart from John Holker, an Englishman late of the Manchester Regiment. Uniforms were modelled upon those of the Royal Ecososis, but with gold hat lace, yellow buttonhole lace on the *justaucorps*, and brass buttons. Unlike the Royal Ecossois, which adopted white breeches at some point after the '45, the Régiment d'Ogilvie appears to have always worn red ones but by the Seven Years War had plain cuffs rather than having the buttoned cuff flaps sported by the Royal Ecossois.

The composition of the Régiment d'Ogilvie was rather more Scottish than was the case for the Régiment d'Albany, and the grenadier company seems to have been entirely composed of Scots. In the fusilier companies, however, over half of the rank and file appear to have been French or German, albeit that an attempt at some point was made to doctor the lists to try and pass them off as Scottish and thus allow the regiment a justification for its continued existence. It is suggested that this was a deliberate fiction, contrived by the officers and by the Ministry of War, in order to keep up the regiment and thus provide a home and pension for the Scots Jacobite exiles.[7] The same logic seems to have been the reason why the Royal Ecossois was retained long after its non-commissioned ranks had also ceased to be other than notionally Scots. Only towards the end of the Seven Years War were the two regiments finally disbanded, their remaining men being drafted into the Irish infantry. Lord Ogilvie, who by this time had risen to the rank of *maréchal de camp*, remained in France until 1778 when he at last received a pardon that allowed him to return home.

---

7   McCorry, 'Rats, Lice and Scotsmen', pp.28-30.

By this stage, too, cut off from its primary source of recruits, the Irish Brigade was also much reduced. The Régiment de Lally had gone out to India with its colonel when he was made Governor General of France's colonies there, and was disbanded upon its return in 1762. The Régiment de Fitzjames was also disbanded in 1762, after being near annihilated in the fighting at Graebenstein on 24 June of that year. The remaining five infantry regiments continued as they were until 1775 when they were cut down to only three – Dillon, Walsh (the former Rooth), and Berwick. They continued to provide a home for the last of the Franco-Irish military families, and for a few Franco-Scots too – Napoleon's *Maréchal* Macdonald, the son of a Jacobite exile, began his career in the Régiment de Dillon – but were increasingly employed in the colonies or on other peripheral operations. When the Revolution came they were incorporated into the regular French line – except for the 2nd Battalion of Dillon, which was in the West Indies and declared for the royalists – and the history of the Irish Brigade came to an end.

If the Irish Brigade lasted until 1791, however, its last decades saw it a shadow of its old self. The hard fighting of the 1740s ripped the heart out of the old core of Jacobite exiles and genuine Irish volunteers, and the collapse of Jacobitism after the '45 and the efforts of the British Government to crack down on French recruitment in Ireland meant that it could not be rebuilt. The French Government certainly showed some gratitude in allowing the Irish and Scots regiments to continue for as long as they did in order to provide for their officers, but even that was a finite provision that slowly dwindled as money became tight in the 1760s and 1770s. For all the good service that the men of the Irish Picquets, Régiment de Fitzjames, and Royal Ecossois did during the Rising of 1745, that year was in many ways the last hurrah of the Irish Brigade, just as it was of the cause for which they fought and died.

# Notes on the Plates

**Plate 1 Naval and Miscellaneous Troops**

A Compagnie de Maurepas
This figure is based on the description given by the Dutch Ambassador van Hoey, for which see Chapter 1. The cut of the hussar-style jacket is based on those worn by the infantry of the Volontaires Bretons who wore a similar uniform.

B and B1 Sailors
Ordinary sailors had no official uniform; the figures in the colour plates are based on typical nautical fashions of the era, with the colour combinations typical of those seen in depictions of French naval dockyards in the mid-18th century, and could represent a crewman from a regular commissioned warship or from one of the many privateers employed to support operations in Scotland.

C Officer of Engineers
This officer wears the uniform as laid out in February 1744, which would have been worn in Scotland by *Chef de Brigade* Mirabelle and *Capitaine* du Saussay.

D Artilleryman
This figure wears the full uniform with *justaucorps*; when serving the guns, the men typically fought in their sleeved waistcoats.

**Plate 2 Irish Troops Part 1**

A *Caporal*, Régiment de Dillon
This junior NCO wears the standard regimental uniform, with his rank indicated by the yellow wool lacing around his cuff buttonholes.

B *Fusilier*, Régiment de Lally, Marching Order
This soldier wears full marching kit, with the *havresac ordinaire* containing rations and personal possessions suspended by a strap over the right shoulder.

Soldiers in a mess took it in turns to carry items of communal kit: in this case the *marmite*, or cooking pot.

C *Fusilier*, Régiment de Rooth, Fatigue Dress
When off duty, or engaged in heavy work, soldiers dispensed with the cocked hat and *justaucorps*. The former was replaced by the *bonnet de police* or forage cap, as shown here.

D *Sérgent*, Régiment de Berwick
As well as metallic lace around the top of his cuffs – in this case, silver – the *sergent*'s badge of rank was his *pertuisan* (head detail shown as D1).

## Plate 3 Irish Troops Part 2

A *Capitaine*, Régiment de Rooth
As a *capitaine*, this officer carries a spontoon as his badge of rank. Note that the waistcoat is laced, but not the *justaucorps*.

B *Tambour*, Régiment de Dillon
The Régiment de Dillon is the only Irish Brigade unit for which we have a reasonable idea of what the dress of the *tambour*s was. Red and black were the livery colours of the Dillon family, whose coat of arms is carried on the drum case, surrounded by decorative cannon and flags.

C *Maître*, Regiment de Fitzjames, on Mounted Duty
This cavalry trooper wears the full uniform of the regiment, but not the iron cuirass (C1) which is unlikely to have been worn in Scotland due to the poor quality of the available horses.

D *Maître*, Regiment de Fitzjames, Dismounted
This cavalryman is shown dismounted, wearing only the buff-leather smallclothes which were standard attire for all French regiments of the *cavalerie légère*. The clumsy riding boots were retained for dismounted duty even by those men issued with infantry muskets to fight on foot in Scotland.

## Plate 4 Royal Ecossois

A Officer with Colour
This officer carries the regimental *drapeau d'ordonnance*; along with the colonel's colour, which had the same design on an all-white ground, these were the only French standards carried in Scotland.

B Officer of Grenadiers
Grenadier officers – and, in theory, subalterns of fusilier companies as well – were to equip themselves for campaign with a musket and bayonet, as shown here, with a belly-box or *gargoussier* to carry ammunition.

C Lord John Drummond in Modified Uniform

Although the locally recruited *Lieutenant* Oliphant is recorded as having worn something similar, only Lord John Drummond is confirmed as having worn the modified uniform shown here with Scots bonnet and cut-down coat.

D Grenadier

The only grenadiers to serve in Scotland belonged to the Royal Ecossois. Equipment was largely as per the fusiliers, but with a curved sabre rather than the lighter, straight-bladed, epée.

Livingstone of Bachuil, Alistair, Christian W.H. Allen, and Betty Stuart Hart (eds.) *Muster Roll of Prince Charles Edward Stuart's Army 1745-46* (Aberdeen: Aberdeen University Press, 1984)

McCorry, Helen C., 'Rats, Lice and Scotchmen: Scottish Infantry Regiments in the Service of France', 1742-62, *JSAHR*, Vol.LXXIV No.297 (Spring 1996), pp.1-38

McLynn, F.J., *France and the Jacobite Rising of 1745* (Edinburgh: Edinburgh University Press, 1981)

McLynn, Frank, *The Jacobite Army in England 1745: The Final Campaign* (Edinburgh: John Donald, 1998)

O'Calaghan, John Cornelius, *History of the Irish Brigades in the Service of France* (Glasgow: Cameron and Ferguson, 1885)

O'Conor, Matthew, *Military History of the Irish Nation, Comprising a Memoir of the Irish Brigade in the Service of France; with an Appendix of Offial papers Relative to the Brigade, from the Archives in Paris* (Dublin: Hodges and Smith, 1845)

Ó Hannracháin, Eoghan, 'An analysis of the Fitzjames Cavalry Regiment, 1737', *The Irish Sword*, Vol.XIX (1993-95), pp.253-276

O'Sullivan, John William (Alistair Tayler and Henriette Tayler eds.), *1745 and After* (London: Thomas Nelson, 1938)

Oates, Jonathan, 'The Manchester Regiment of 1745', *JSAHR*, Vol.88, No.354 (Summer 2010), pp.129-151

Petard, Michel, *Equipements Militaires de 1600 a 1870, Tome I 1600 à 1750* (Privately Published, 1986)

Riding, Jacqueline, *Jacobites. A New History of the '45 Rebellion* (London: Bloomsbury, 2016)

Reid, Stuart, *1745. A Military History of the Last Jacobite Rising* (Staplehurst: Spellmount, 1996)

Reid, Stuart, *Like Hungry Wolves. Culloden Moor 16 April 1746* (London: Windrow and Green, 1994)

Reid, Stuart, *The Scottish Jacobite Army 1745-46* (Oxford: Osprey, 2006)

Seton, Brevet-Colonel Sir Bruce (ed.), *The Orderly Book of Lord Ogilvie's Regiment in the Army of Prince Charles Edward Stuart 10 October, 1745, to 21 April, 1746* (Heaton Mersey: The Cloister Press for the Society of Army Historical Research, 1923)

Seton, Sir Bruce Gordon, and Jean Gordon Arnot, *Prisoners of the '45* (Edinburgh: Edinburgh University Press for the Scottish History Society, 3 Vols., 1928-1929)

Wood, Stephen, 'An Officer's Mitre Cap of *Le Regiment Royal-Ecossois*, 1745', *JSAHR*, Vol.LXXV No.302 (Summer 1997), pp.77-83.

Zimmermann, Doron, *The Jacobite Movement in Scotland and in Exile, 1746-1759* (Basingstoke: Palgrave Macmillan, 2003)

## Online Sources

*Three Decks – Warships in the Age of Sail*, at www.threedecks.org.